My Face to the World

JOY BROWN

ISBN: 1-4392-4532-0
ISBN-13: 9781439245323

Visit www.booksurge.com to order additional copies.

Dedication

This book is dedicated to my mom, who I wish was here to be able to read it and to "Miracle Ed", who was my inspiration-I miss them both always. And to all whose lives have been touched in any way by cancer.

Chapter 1

A cancer diagnosis is a private matter. Does that statement surprise you? It does me too. I was diagnosed with breast cancer on May 31, 2002. My summer and beyond was full of people. Doctors, nurses, friends, family, strangers, a myriad of them. But I was alone really and I was the only one who knew, out of all of those people, how it all felt, for me. How it felt to find something wrong, to go through the testing, to have false hope given to me, then taken away. How it felt to have part of my body taken- to be changed forever by that. To be told "I have some tough news for you." *To never be the same person again.* I was the one who endured the treatments, the surgeries, felt the fear. Life would never again be as I expected it to be. But I digress, and here is my story.

I was going through life at age 44 just like most people. Working, raising kids, stressing about life, money or lack of it. All the normal stuff. I was working part time in an office, not a lot of hours, but it gave me a little extra money and some time away from the house. In the spring of 2002 I started having some shooting pains through my right breast. At first I really didn't think anything of it. People have shooting pains all of the time. This one persisted and was always in the same place. I couldn't get it out of my head. One day a voice in my head just told me to check it out. So I, for some reason, reached up and went right to what felt like a lump. I was shocked. Didn't think I was really feeling anything. Thought it must be my imagination. It took a couple days of the pain still being there and me not being able to get it all out of my head for me to call my doctor. I called her from the privacy of my office at work. She got me an appointment for a couple hours from when I called.

I got off work and went home. I had about an hour and a half to kill. I thought I was okay. I was SO wrong. I had a meltdown. That's the only way to describe it. I didn't call and tell my husband. Why should I? I didn't want to worry him over what would probably-no definitely- turn out to be nothing. So I called my older sister. She lives in a town about thirty miles from me-the town I grew up in. She was at work and I am sure she heard the panic in my voice. She dropped everything and met me at the radiologists.

I got in and had to fill out papers. "Why are you here today?" was one question. You don't know how much I wish I could have marked 'routine mammogram'. No, I had to mark. FOUND A LUMP. Who put me into this nightmare and how did I get out?

As medical offices go, I waited for what seemed like forever to be called back. I wanted to hear my name, wanted to not hear it, wanted to run out the door. I finally got called back. They took picture after picture and kept coming back for more. I counted thirteen total views taken. I would sit and wait and I was able to hear the tech and the radiologist talking. You would think that they would try to avoid that. He was telling her he needed more of not only the right breast but the left one, too. He saw something in there that I had not felt yet. So now, not only were they checking out the lump I felt, but something He saw too. Anxiety level-appropriately increased.

After the pictures, I had an ultrasound of the breasts. This gives them a better view of things. They are supposed to be able to tell if the lumps are solid-possibly cancerous, or liquid-cysts and what you pray for if you have the choice. After that I waited in a little room for them to tell me what they found. The tech comes in and tells me I am free to go home, that what I felt and what he saw were indeed, just cysts.

Overjoyed? Of course. Relieved? Obviously. I went out and told my sister. She hugged me goodbye. Little did I know at the time, when she hugged me, she felt that this was far from over.

Chapter 2

The routine of normal life did not return after I got my so-called good news. I learned many times to trust my instincts-that when that voice in my head spoke to me, I had better listen. This was one of those times. I KNEW it wasn't over, I KNEW it was not just a cyst. And as much as I wanted to be happy and to believe it, I just couldn't. It was also pretty hard to ignore because as each day passed, it was growing bigger.

I was very lucky, in that I was scheduled for my yearly checkup with my regular doctor shortly after my visit to the radiologists. When she checked out the lump and the size she asked me if I wanted to go see the surgeon to see about getting it removed, because even a cyst like that doesn't belong in the body. Of course, I wanted it out. Maybe then I could quit thinking about it.

She called down to the surgeon's office to schedule an appointment. Wouldn't you know, he was on vacation and wouldn't be back for two weeks. So the appointment was made for May 30th. The days dragged by, my nephew graduated. (I look at me in those pictures from that weekend and see the old me, the one I will never know again.)

Appointment day finally came.

I went alone as I was not expecting anything bad to occur. The doctor came in and checked things out. He had to show a couple of his students this rather large cyst. He said "Let's get this thing drained and get you on your way home!"

But a funny thing happened on my way home-we hit a BIG detour. As the doctor was trying to drain the cyst, nothing came out, at least no liquid. When he saw a little tissue and blood, he said "This is not good. We are going to change gears here".

I was suddenly being prepared for a biopsy. I wanted to jump off the table and to run faster and further than I had ever run in my life. I didn't want to do this. Not THIS.

I won't describe the procedure...needless to say it was not fun. When he got done, he said to me, "I don't expect to make a diagnosis of breast cancer because most breast cancers grow very slowly and this seems to have grown very fast. I will call you tomorrow with the results."

So I got to go home and wait. The next morning, I went to work like any other day, jumping when the phone rang. I got done and went home and paced. And paced. And paced. Finally the phone rang at 4:10 p.m. (yes I remember the exact time.) It was the doctor on the other end. Which I immediately knew was bad news. After all, if it were good news, he would just let the nurse call me.

Then I heard the words that would forever change my life.

"I have some tough news for you."

Suddenly it was like I was in a vacuum; I could only hear parts of the rest of the conversation. I heard 'fast-growing' and 'aggressive' and something about being in his office the next Monday to talk about what we were going to do. I was sobbing; begging him to please tell me it wasn't true. He asked if my husband was there and if he could talk to him. I handed Tom the phone-well not even handed, exactly. I walked up to the dining room table where he was sitting and slid it over to him and walked away hoping that the kids couldn't hear me. I couldn't quit crying.

To know Tom, you would know that he rarely sheds a tear over anything, but this time was different. When he hung up the phone he came to me and we hugged. We said nothing at the time. There was really nothing that could be said or really needed to be said then. I just needed to have him hold me and let me cry.

After that, I called everyone I knew. I know some people don't like anyone to know. I needed for many to know. I believe strongly in the power of prayer. You see the day I got my diagnosis, my uncle who had been battling cancer and not given much hope, had got the word he was cancer free. He became the one I looked to for inspiration.

The toughest call I had to make was to my mom. I told her and she had only two words, two very sad words the way she said them. "Oh Joy."

Chapter 3

The weekend of June 2-3, 2002 was the longest, shortest weekend in my life. I wanted it to end. I wanted it to never end. I wanted to get this cancer out of me as soon as possible, but I didn't want to go through everything that meant. And understand, at this time, it was ALL unknown to me. The pathology, the prognosis, the course of treatment. Everything. The doctor called on a Friday afternoon, late. My appointment with him wasn't until three days later on a Monday afternoon late. So he gave me the gift and the curse of three days before my life turned into the whirlwind of appointments and doctors. It was already thrown into turmoil; there was no waiting period for that.

That weekend I lost six pounds. I could not eat anything. This diet, I don't recommend to anyone! I couldn't sleep. It wasn't that I didn't want to. *I couldn't.* The night, the dark, was so hard. The doctor's voice would resonate over and over in my head. All I would hear was "I have some tough news for you. I have some tough news for you. I HAVE SOME TOUGH NEWS FOR YOU!" It wouldn't stop.

That Saturday morning normally was my Saturday to work. I had already called them Friday night to tell them the news. I told them I would be back when I could. But not now. Not with so many uncertainties ahead of me. I took my two youngest to the North Iowa Band Festival. It's just what it says it is and it is a very big deal here. Meredith Wilson of the Music Man fame grew up here and started it. We have a big parade and lots of people come and have fun. I usually had to miss this kind of stuff because I was always working. I decided I wanted to take the kids. They questioned me why I wasn't working. I said I took the day off. Not a lie. I could not tell them the whole truth just yet. I had to go to my doctor's appointment first and hear what he would have to tell me.

As I sat watching the parade, I mostly watched all the women going by. I wanted to see just one who knew what I was feeling. One who was a survivor. But no matter how hard I looked, I could not tell. No one was walking around with I AM A BREAST CANCER SURVIVOR on their shirt. I felt alone.

Monday came finally. It came too soon. Tom and I went to my appointment. It surprised me how easily I could cry in front of strangers. It was like I was outside myself listening to all this. I had a large over 5 cm tumor. Shut up. It was aggressive and fast growing. Shut up. I would have to have a mastectomy because of its size and aggressiveness. PLEASE JUST SHUT UP! He also was sure because of all this I would have to have two rounds of chemotherapy and two rounds of radiation. That scared me more than the surgery itself. I could only agree though, to it all, because I already had decided to do everything I could to survive this. Here I was only 44 years old with four young children, thinking about what I had to do to simply stay alive and be here for them.

I had overcome many things in my life. I became a fighter and survivor out of necessity. My father died when I was only four and for all rights and purposes I grew up without one. My mom remarried to a man I never did get along with. It was a difficult life at best. After school, I just wanted out of the house, so I tried so many schools and jobs, just not knowing what to do. I never had the guidance and never had anyone who gave me the confidence to know how to follow my dreams. When I married, it was whirlwind. I met him in May, we married in December, had our first child in June. He was wonderful, did things so soon, so we decided to try to have another. Our second son was born less than two years after the first. It didn't take long to learn he was not like the other one. He had a difficult birth, and now he had a disability. We have encountered many fights through the years for him. We always win. When he was five, he unlocked the door, got out, and was picked up by a stranger who took him to the police station. There they called the Department of Human Services. They put me on a child abuse registry. I was outraged. I fought the laws and a few years later after much hard work my name was removed and the laws were changed. Another battle won.

I knew I had had many battles before this one. I had fought them. I had won. I didn't plan on this one being any different. I knew it in my heart that I would be okay. I knew I would literally go through Hell first but I kept my eye on the other side to when I knew it would all be over.

The surgeon had to coordinate schedules with the plastic surgeon. I had opted for immediate reconstruction. I was only 44 and wanted to at least look normal to the outside world. I had to wait for yet another appointment.

We decided we had to tell the kids when we got home. We picked McDonald's up on the way home. It was so hard to sit there knowing that I had to soon shatter their safe young world. It was not near as hard as finding the words to actually tell them.

We called them into the living room. Chris, our oldest at 16, was sitting in the chair. Jamie, 14 was in his room, I told him later, not knowing how much he could really understand of it all. Daniel, 12 was standing by his dad. Kayla, my one and only daughter and youngest at age 10 was sitting on the couch beside me.

So I simply told them. I had breast cancer. Not a big reaction from Chris. He told me he already had it all figured out. He was in tune. He had been listening. Daniel's knees buckled. His dad had to catch him. He started to cry. Kayla my baby, started to sob. I cannot tell you how it feels to hurt your children in this way. To tell them THEIR world will never be the same either. Kayla asked me if I was going to die. I told her NO! I felt it. I said to them. I will be fine. I felt that too. It was just something I knew. I also told them. "God gave me you guys as children for a reason. You are very special. And we will all get through this together." I hugged them and told them I loved them. And my heart felt like it was shattering into tiny little pieces that I just didn't know how to gather and find the way to put back together again.

Chapter 4

Waiting. One of the hardest things to do. And something I had to do a lot. Wait for appointments, wait for results. Waiting.

I finally got to see the plastic surgeon. I, of course, would have preferred to do that the same day I saw the surgeon to get it over with and get on with things, but in the real world it doesn't happen like that. My sister went with me to the consultation for moral support. While we sat in the waiting room we laughed and told jokes. Here I was, just having been diagnosed with cancer, waiting to see one of the surgeons that was going to alter the body God had given me. And what was I doing? LAUGHING! It felt good. I could see the receptionist looking at us. So what? My sister made a joke about the doctor being "Jason, the Mason City, chain saw wielding boob remover." A crass joke? I didn't care. It made me laugh.

I got called back. There was the doctor, his nurse and a nurse from the cancer center in there. The last one was sitting in for the new case manager of the breast care center. (That center is a wonderful place. They follow you from diagnosis through treatment and beyond. I still see the director to this day and consider her a friend.)

If you ever had a baby you know how all dignity goes right out the window. I decided standing there with my boobs hanging out for the world to see that between this and the babies, ALL my dignity was now gone. Your body is private? HA! Try to tell the medical field that.

I was, as they say, rather 'well-endowed.' My plastic surgeon told me when they took the breast with cancer he would at least have to do a reduction in the other. What he recommended was a bilateral mastectomy-I had dense breasts with cysts and it would be a smart thing to prevent something like this happening with the remaining one. I agreed to it. He sent me on my way. To yes, wait some more for him and the other surgeon to coordinate schedules for surgery because after one took them off, the other would start to build them back up.

Do I regret agreeing to have both removed? Intellectually-no. Emotionally-all the time. Sometimes yes I miss them, but more on that later.

Before I had to go under the knife they had to do a biopsy on the cyst in the left one. Yes another biopsy. I went alone to this one. I prayed of course that when he put the needle in he would be draining it. I watched the whole thing on ultrasound. And to my relief, it did drain. I was still nervous waiting for the results. The nurse finally called me. You know what that means then. No cancer. The nurses get to call with the good news.

I had various other routine tests for surgery. Blood work, chest x-ray (don't want to find anything there). A physical at my regular doctors. She is a great doctor. She was truly heartbroken over what I found out. And shocked. (SHE was?!)

I finally got the call that I would have surgery on June 12th. Finally a firm date. Not soon enough for me. I had a hard time sleeping. I keep thinking, What if one more day is one too many? Wonder if that day was the day it decided to move to other parts of my body. I wanted the cancer out and I wanted it out NOW! I tried to will it to shrink. I did a lot of sitting out on the deck with my eyes closed, meditating. My husband would try to touch me. I wouldn't let him. I felt impure somehow. I just couldn't feel good about my body for any reason at that time. I knew it would never ever be the same again. I was trying to deal with that and having a very hard time.

June 12th finally arrived. One of my sisters came to the house around 8 a.m., which was about two hours before I had to leave for the hospital. If she was looking for conversation she found none. I had gone inside myself much earlier that day and did not want to talk. I had a lot on my mind. I needed to be silent for me.

The time finally arrived to leave. I hugged and kissed the kids goodbye and got in the car. That was very difficult. We arrived and my oldest sister and mom were there already waiting for us.

I got checked in and Tom and Jo, my oldest sister got to go to the surgery prep area with me. We still joked and waited and waited and waited. The doctors both came in and did some prep. The plastic surgeon drew all over me and the other surgeon put his initials on the side where the cancer was. One of the nurses popped her head in-she happened to have been a media teacher when my husband was in high school. And she was also a breast cancer survivor. I still talk to her to this day.

The time came to go. I of course had an iv already in my arm. I thought I would get wheeled down to the operating room. I was wrong. I had to carry the bag and walk down to the room. I couldn't help but think of the movie Dead Man Walking. I got in the room and looked around at all the instruments, the nurses running around and reality was really starting to sink in. It wasn't a dream, a nightmare yes, but a real one. I got up on the table, they strapped down my arms. The anesthetist started his thing. I was out. When I woke up it would be all over and I would no longer be the same person who climbed onto that table a few hours before.

Chapter 5

"Joy?" Squeeze my fingers. Coming out of anesthesia is not a fun feeling. It is very disorienting when you try to wake up from such a deep sleep.

I barely was starting to open my eyes. I could vaguely make out the image of the nurse over me. I glanced at the clock behind her. I think it was 5:40 at night or close to it. I just remember thinking it was a lot later than the last time I had my eyes open.

I didn't want to squeeze her fingers, I just wanted to close my eyes again. But I obliged and then again when she asked me to.

"Good". Heard her make a phone call to tell someone I was awake. It wasn't but minutes later, it seemed, that I was already on my way to my room. When I got there my family wasn't there yet as they wanted me to get in my bed first. They actually asked me if I was able to get off the table from the recovery room and into the bed by myself. Who were they kidding? Oh sure if I wanted to not only scream out in pain but also end up on the floor. They got some help and got me into bed. Getting moved was my first taste of the pain that was to come.

They had me on a morphine drip for the pain. I immediately asked for something else. It made the room spin a lot and I hated how it made me feel. They obligingly put me on oral pain meds. I was to ask for them whenever I needed them. I told them to keep them coming.

My family was notified that I was back in my room. They were all there and they all came in. They swore later that I wouldn't remember anything going on or who was there. They were wrong. I remembered it all. Even an unpleasant scene happening across the hall. Most of them only stayed long enough to see that I was okay and alive still. Tom stayed longer but also eventually left too so that I could sleep. Which is funny when you think about it. I was in the hospital, who lets you sleep there?

They wanted me to get up walking by 9 or 10 that night. I on the other hand thought that was just a wee bit early. But you know at some point you have to go to the bathroom so it was time to see how I was on my feet. I didn't do too badly. It was the middle of the night by now, much later than the 9 or 10 that they were going to get me walking. My nurse sat down and told me she knew how I was feeling because she had had the same operation. YES! Someone I could relate to. She asked me if it felt like an elephant was sitting on my chest. I replied yes. Because I imagine that IF an elephant was sitting on my chest this is exactly how much it would hurt. She stayed and chatted awhile. I tried to sleep. It didn't happen.

The next day my room was full of visitors and flowers and more flowers and more flowers. My other sister came to see me and she was so funny giving one of the guys who was either a male nurse or an orderly or such all kinds of instructions. I did get another table put in for all the flowers that kept coming. I was surprised at the love that was pouring out. To look at the beauty of the flowers there and all that they stood for, the love, the well wishes, it helped me to feel better, to smile.

On the first full day in the hospital something very interesting happened. Before I tell you this, it needs just a little back story.

At this time Jamie's home room special education teacher was a girl from my hometown. She was a year behind me in school. When I was in third grade and she was in second grade we had our tonsils out and shared a hospital room. While I woke up and threw up blood and had to stay a little longer, she was fine and went on her way home before me.

In the spring of 2002 we had an IEP meeting for Jamie. For those of you that don't know that is an Individualized Education Plan where we discuss his goals and how to achieve them. Kim was telling me that she was not going to teach summer school because she was having major surgery and jokingly she said to me, why don't you have surgery too so I know I will get out of the hospital fast. Ha ha, right?

I walk out of my door to take a walk in the hallway and who do they wheel by but Kim herself. I chuckled. I told the nurses, you let me know when she is awake. I need to make a visit. Later in the day they told me she was awake and sitting up. I decided it was time for a walk. I went down the hallway and walked into her room. You should have seen the look on her face! JOY! What are you doing here? So I told her. And I reminded her of what she said at the IEP meeting. Told her next time she was going to have surgery, please leave me out of it. I was glad we could laugh about it, but the irony of it all never left me.

Hospital stays are pretty much the same, you don't sleep they wake you up for vitals all the time, you know the drill. I went in on a

Wednesday and was supposed to go home on a Friday. But Friday afternoon about the time I was going to be going my sister told me I didn't look too good. Well, truth be told, I didn't feel too good. I had managed to spike a fever. Doctor was called and I was their guest for yet another night. I was happy and sad about that. I wanted to go home to my family but afraid to go home and have to deal with things.

Like the drains. I didn't tell you about those yet. I had one put in each side-drain tubes literally sewed into me connecting to a container to collect the blood. Drainage would normally last a week or two. I had to measure, keep track , write it down, etc. If I wanted to go anywhere I had to make sure they were hooked to the inside of my shirts. I didn't let them slow me down though. I walked around outside. Did what I normally did. They were just a temporary inconvenience. I was back at the plastic surgeons on the Tuesday after I got out of the hospital to have them removed already. To say that was a relief was an understatement.

During surgery they also removed 9 of my lymph nodes under my right arm. The purpose of that is to check to see if the cancer had spread. So guess what? More waiting for results of which could decide my future or lack of it. I didn't find out until later that the doctor was very worried when he removed them. He didn't like the looks of them at all. When he went in and talked to my family after surgery he as much told them so. And he had other news too. The tumor was even a little bigger 5.2 cm. (See it just kept growing.) To put that in perspective to those who don't know, a normal size breast cancer tumor is only 1-2 cm. Not good. (Oh and the reason they thought it was a cyst and not a tumor? The tumor was totally surrounded by cysts, so when they did they ultrasound the cysts hid the tumor.) The other part that concerned him-it was within ONE MILLEMETER of my chest muscle. Seems I was right to worry about just one more day......My sister told me that my husband became very pale when he heard all of the news. She thought he would faint. To this day he does not recall anything the doctor said in that room.

When they remove lymph nodes they usually end up damaging nerves. You know that tingly feeling you sometimes get when your foot is asleep? That is what I live with now and will have for the rest of my life. I am now at a high risk to develop Lymph edema so I have to be very cautious. A scratch , a bug bite, can all mean trouble. An airplane? Have to wear a compression sleeve. I try not to let it interfere too much with my everyday life. But it is my right arm and I am right handed so it is something I am constantly dealing with.

Are you wondering what I found out? Well the DOCTOR called me with the results. Did my heart stop? Because you remember I said the doctor only calls with bad news?? This time after all I had already been through; HE wanted to be the one to give me some good news. ALL of the nodes were negative. There was NO sign of metastatic disease. It had not spread. Prayers DO work. These had been answered. I knew from this very moment when I got the news that no matter what, from now on I could do this. I just had to get through the next few months and I would be back to my life. I was going to win another fight!

Chapter 6

Right before I went to the hospital for surgery, I bought a new recliner. I knew I wasn't going to be sleeping in my bed and needed somewhere comfortable to sleep. I never knew I would spend 6 weeks sleeping in that recliner. I tried to sleep in my bed after a couple weeks, on my back, which was really difficult since I am a side sleeper. That didn't work and back to the chair I went. I bought large body pillows hoping that I could sleep with those alongside me. That didn't work either. And back to the recliner I went.

The first of July came. I drove again for the first time since surgery. It was a bit painful but liberating. I didn't feel so much like a prisoner anymore. I went to get groceries, but had to take Chris and Kayla to lift anything. It was so hard to have to rely on them.They had been called upon so much in their young lives to help out and they never complained. How did I get so blessed? It was so hard to have to rely on anyone much less your young children. No one knew how much it bothered me to not be able to lift laundry, groceries or do pretty much anything. I was dependent on a lot of people. And I hated it fiercely. My whole life I took care of people from my siblings, to babysitting, to having kids of my own. I liked being a caretaker. I did not like be the one being taken care of. Unfortunately there was much more of that to come.

When I had returned from the hospital we had people come in bringing us meals for the whole family. I was very humbled. But probably no more than one day when the phone rang. It was someone I had never met wanting to bring us food. She brought out a ham, some cheese, come cupcakes for the kids. I cannot tell you how that made me feel.

Treatment had to start within 4 weeks of surgery. On July 2nd I had to go to the Cancer Center to meet my oncologist. (I had actually got a letter saying WELCOME to the Cancer Center. I don't know about you, but that was one welcome I could have done without!)

This was one of those visits I call a slap in your face reality visits. You can sit there and listen to all they say TO you, ABOUT you, but find it so hard to believe you are there at all. My oncologist was wonderful. I cannot say enough good things about this man. He came into the room and treated Tom and I with the utmost respect.

I felt that I really mattered to him and wasn't just another cancer case sitting in front of him. That mattered to me.

He told me I was a complicated case. My heart sank. But then he said in a GOOD way. Relief. (God this emotional roller coaster was getting to be a tough ride!) The tumor was large as we know and he was surprised all the nodes were negative. He said I would have to have a CAT scan and Bone scans to make sure that the cancer hadn't spread anywhere. Just hearing that scared me more than anything I had heard to date. He did say that he wasn't 'expecting' to find anything. (Didn't I just hear THAT a couple months before?) But even IF he did, the treatment would remain the same. He thought the tumor grew large so fast because of my age and that hormones really feed the cells to grow. He wasn't sure about radiation; he would wait for the scans. I WOULD have 4-6 rounds of chemo. One day of it, then 3 weeks off. I would probably only feel tired but to stay busy, to keep working and doing everything I normally would do. I didn't like to hear that but it was better than what I expected. I figured once a week for months. So I put it in my mind that this would be doable. And then it would be behind me too. I was just looking forward to getting it all done and then helping others through it too. Yes, I had already decided that! I was looking forward to my hair coming back and I hadn't even lost it yet. I was already thinking that it better come back curly if I had to go through all of this horror.

I would have to have a port put in sometime before chemo. Great, more surgery. Little did I know it was only the 2nd surgery of many to come. I agreed to this because it saves the veins during chemo. I had to wait to have that scheduled. Good more waiting. You would think I would be a pro at that by now. I still didn't like it. I didn't have to wait too long. The port would be put in the following Monday at the hospital. Although it is a simple thing to do, we had to have a sterile environment and I would have to have anesthesia.

The day before all my scans was the Fourth of July. I normally worked on holidays so it was unusual I had the day off. We went to my sister's house. They live on Main Street in Clear Lake. There is always a big parade in that town and I got to finally see it. But I didn't enjoy it much. I couldn't quit thinking about the scans I would be having the next day. They were SO important.

Friday morning came. I had to drink some horrible horrible stuff before the scans. At about noon I had to have an injection. That hurt a bit. We had to sit around and wait for awhile after that before I could have the scans. I did some people watching. There was a lot of crying people in the hospital that day. I felt bad for them even though I didn't know what they were going through.

I went in at 2:30 for the bone scan. They strapped me down to a table. It was to take 30 minutes. It felt like three. Somehow I zoned out and went somewhere else for 30 minutes. The person who prepped me said they would look at it again before I went home and if it showed ANYTHING, whether it was arthritis-or worse, they would ask for more x-rays.

I got done there and went and waited a bit to be called back to CT. I had to wait yet another hour since they were running behind. I just wanted to get it all over with. I finally went in there and had to be injected with Iodine. I must be allergic to that because it hurt like Hell! There is no other way to describe it. The CT lasted only about 5 minutes.

Poor Tom, he had to sit in yet another waiting room and wait for me. This was getting to be a habit I didn't like! But we got sent on our way, which was good. I made him stop for pizza on the way home. This mama was hungry!

Time to wait for more test results. It is never ever easy to do that. Time has a way of slowing

way down when you are waiting to hear results.
Sometimes if feels like your worst enemy. It would
be Tuesday before I heard the results.

I got the call. I wanted to scream from
the rooftops. I wanted to tell everyone I knew
and everyone I didn't. Both scans I had were
NORMAL! This rotten disease did not spread!!!
I felt so happy. I tried hard not to cry. But I did
anyhow. I think I deserved some tears of joy.
I knew then I could get through my treatments
and got on with my life.

Chapter 7

Sunday my sister Jayne was up. Since I knew after the first treatment I would be losing my hair, I let her cut my hair short. That was painful in its own way. I had always worn my hair long. I knew cutting it was the right thing to do, that although it would be hard to have my hair come out into my hands, it would be more of a mess if it was long. It felt very strange to have it so short. Wouldn't you know it; I got more compliments on that haircut. I wanted to tell them all to shut up. It was only short because in a couple weeks it would be all gone. They didn't know how painful it was to hear them tell me how much they liked my hair!

Monday came and it was time to go to the hospital to have my port put in. I didn't have to wait for this surgery, they were actually on time. I wasn't even put under. They sedated me, which was horrible. It made me very nauseous. I thought they would never get done. I was awake for the whole surgery. I was back in my room within the hour. Then I promptly got sick.

No surprise to me. Still I drank a little coffee, ate a little toast. An hour later, I went home. I slept for a little while and had a sandwich when I woke up.

I didn't sleep well that night either. The port was put right under my left collarbone, completely under the skin. It looked like a bump if you looked at it. They could access it by putting the needle directly in it. When I would lie on my left side it felt like it was squishing it and it hurt. So now it hurt still to lay on my right side and also on the left. I wasn't much liking having this foreign object in my body. The whole time I had it, it hurt, clothes touching it, hurt. It was never comfortable.

I got word that my first chemo treatment would be on Thursday. I was very nervous about it. You can hear so much on the news about chemotherapy but never know what it must be like to go through it. I was about to find out.

Wednesday, July 10th. Significant? Not really. It was just finally a day with NO appointments. A temporary reprieve, a day to play pretend. Pretend my life was normal. Hey I would take what I could get!

Thursday. D-Day. First chemo. The day I had been dreading for so long. Tom and I went out to breakfast then onto the Cancer Center. They took blood first for a blood count. They had to check that my counts were not too low. If they were, then chemo had to be postponed. That is something I prayed about each time. I did not want this prolonged anymore than it was supposed to take.

They also weighed me. I didn't mind this time, because I had just lost 20 pounds and was where I wanted to be. Little did I know that would be the last time I would be seeing that number! Each time I went the chemo helped put 5 pounds back on. It just kept getting better.

Next it was off to see the doctor. He had to check the blood counts and I had also developed a rash from the antibiotics I took after the surgery to have the port put in. He had to look at that too. Next it was on to the chemo room. So it all had begun.

While you are there you have to chew on shaved ice or something similar. It helps prevent mouth sores. I thought mine was yummy. Strawberry flavored. Guess what, after the first time I was never able to not only eat red colored shaved ice, to not only not be able to even look at it, I was never able even able to talk about it. The kids even know better than to mention it. To this day I have an unpleasant physical reaction to it. Right now talking about it, I can feel my throat tightening, trying to keep the contents of my stomach in place.

When we were done, we went down the hall to the wig closet. For two weeks after the first chemo, you can expect for the hair to start leaving your head. We had so much fun. I would try on everything in there and most were hideous. We laughed so hard. That felt so good. I did find two that would work. One looked very similar to the way I had my hair cut then and was the appropriate color of red.

I was sent home on anti-nausea meds. A couple different kinds. I was thankful for the advances in medicine. I did not want to get violently sick. I don't like to throw up.

From the Cancer Center I went to the plastic surgeon's office. It was the day of my first fill. When he followed the other surgeon the day of the mastectomy, he put expanders behind my muscles. There would be a series of filling those with a saline solution. The tissue and muscles needed to be stretched to make room for the implants.

In the expanders were a little hole or tube that he put the needle in and proceeded to fill. 100cc a time. That was plenty. That hurt. We would go until it was the size, maybe just a little bit bigger than the implants we had picked out. Can you imagine picking out what 'size' you want to be? It would be smaller than I was. Thank goodness. And trust me, never get your husband's opinion- you would look like one of those Hollywood women who are much too large!

The first of both was finally behind me and no longer a mystery. How I would feel in the coming days, now that was the big question!

The day after my first chemo was my first poor me day. No one said that I had to always be happy and positive. This day I definitely wasn't. I was feeling 'mildly yucky' that day. I took my anti-nausea meds and kept a lot of saltines nearby as they seemed to help. I had one of those heads where you just don't feel well-somewhere between dizzy and a headache if that makes sense. I didn't dare cough as it felt like it would be followed by vomiting.

Now for the poor me part-I missed my old life. I missed getting up for work. I missed complaining about it like everyone does. I missed having a clean house and being able to clean it. I missed doing what needed to be done or what I wanted to do. I just missed being me. I still was you say? For those who may have gone through this they know what it is to look into a mirror and see a stranger. This is what it feels like. Sometimes I felt like a stranger in my own skin. Yes, I knew it was all temporary and that someday it would be all behind me. But yes, I got angry once in awhile. I was angry it happened to me. I was angry I had to do this now. I was angry that my children's safe world was shattered and that they would never ever get that feeling of security back again.

The next day my oldest sister, Jo came and picked me up and took me to Charles City for the weekend. Their Relay for Life was that weekend. I did not walk; I could barely walk a few feet as it was. My younger sister, Jayne came too. I watched them walk along the track that was lined with luminaries-bags with names of those who we had lost to cancer, my aunt was one of them, and those of us who were battling it or had in the past-the survivors. My name was there along with another aunt, an uncle and a cousin. I was overcome with the emotion of it. Sitting there alone looking at all those bags with names of loved ones, I cried. The survivors walk was also very powerful. It was led by a school mate of mine and her young son. He had been diagnosed with leukemia three days before I was diagnosed with cancer. Suddenly someone with whom I had nothing in common with in high school became my friend. It was funny how common tragedy can bring even strangers together.

I watched the survivors walk. I longed for the next year when I would be one of them. A survivor. God that sounded great! A SURVIVOR. Yes, that was me too!

Chapter 8

It was the first Monday after my first chemo treatment. I was feeling extremely tired. I had no energy. I thought I could return to work then, but I needed a bit more time. I had a lot of light-headedness that wouldn't go away. I tried sleeping in three different places but could not get comfortable. I yearned for just one good night's sleep. I was glad I didn't feel any worse than I did. I couldn't imagine how people did this when they had to do it day after day. I don't know if I could.

This was not an easy thing to be doing. I also could not imagine what it was like to be one of the ones on the outside watching it happen to me. I only knew what it felt like to be me. I know both positions are tough ones to be in. I was trying to get back to normal a bit-whatever that meant-for my family.

Tuesday. Things were pretty much the same. The nurse from the Cancer Center called to check on me. She thought the light-headedness came from the Decadron I was taking for nausea and that when I got that out of my system that the feeling should go away. I hoped so. It was rather annoying. It was hard to do anything with that feeling in your head. I wasn't sure when I would feel like returning to work, but knew some normalcy for everyone, and of course a paycheck would be nice again.

Wednesday I was feeling a little bit better. I was still light headed when I moved wrong. Baby steps. But then my head had started to tingle. It was the sign of the baldy to come. Rats! I could not imagine in my worst nightmare what that was going to be like.

Even though my doctor had called and left me a message that my scan results were in, I got a letter from him saying they were normal with no sign of metastatic disease. It is always good to get every little bit of positive that you can. Especially in the middle of feeling so crappy.

By Thursday one week after treatment, the light-headedness was better, but my bones hurt. The ached through and through. I didn't know bones could hurt so much. It made it hard to get comfortable. I noticed a few bruises popping up here and there, which was no surprise considering the attack going on in my body at the time.

Tom surprised me by taking a half day off. He took me to my next fill and out to Wal-Mart for groceries. I was glad they had benches because a simple trip to the grocery story wore me out.

Friday and I was finally feeling pretty good. My head felt good and my bones didn't hurt. It was so nice to feel almost normal. And I had no appointments until the next Friday for a follow-up with the surgeon. It was a good day.

Sunday I had one of those moments again. Most days I didn't dwell on what happened to me, because what would be the point? It is a fact and it happened for a reason. That I never questioned. But human nature is that sometimes we do ask why or get mad at what is happening to us. Something just happened that threw it all in my face. I was not the same person that I was. Physically or otherwise. And it was very strange for me. My whole life was different. Now that wasn't always a bad thing, but for me now it was just a fact. As time went by I knew things would get back to a more normal life, but still would never again be the same. Life has a way of slapping you in the face and giving you that wake up call, doesn't it? I knew, at any rate, that life went on. Good or bad. I chose to think good. Always. No matter what has happened to me I always look at the glass at being half full. What about yours?

Tuesday July 23rd, I finally returned to work. It was great to be back. Everyone was glad to see me. I only wish I could have got them to look at my eyes and not elsewhere to see how 'different' I now looked. They did the nicest thing. They had a potluck and had a cake to welcome me back. I was humbled yet again. I dared to feel that little bit of normalcy returning. It felt good.

I was finally sleeping in my bed, Kayla started clarinet lessons, I was working again, school was starting soon, and it was all good.

Then it started.

Friday July 26, 2002. The hair started coming out. I did not like it one bit. It was so hard to imagine it all gone. I didn't want to. I wanted it to stop. But there was nothing I could do to prevent what was now happening to me. I know it was only hair, but go stand in front of the mirror and imagine it all gone. I know it meant the chemo was killing cells in my body if any had escaped that tumor. But did it have to kill these cells too?

It is not easy combing your hair and seeing a bunch of it in your comb or brush. It was gradual over the weekend. A little more each day. I wore a hat. Each day it came out faster. Each time I would touch my head; there was hair in my hand. My heart was hurting, breaking. I had a moment when I thought, How am I supposed to feel like a woman? They took my breasts and now I am losing my hair. It was a difficult thing to deal with.

By Monday the hair was coming out in handfuls. It was depressing. Could I go yet another day before the inevitable? I did. Tuesday morning I got up. If you ever had one of those dolls in the old days you know how matted the hair gets. That was me. It looked horrible. It no longer even looked like hair. Tom had teased and said he wanted to shave my head so badly. So I let him. And when it came right down to doing it, it wasn't so easy for him. He didn't like having my hair in his hands. And oh was it so hard. I cried a couple times while he was shaving my head. I made him hand me a baseball cap right away. I went into the bedroom and put on the wig I bought. I could not look at myself in the mirror. I did not want to see hairless me. I would not be able to look in the mirror for several weeks. I now looked like a cancer patient and I didn't want to see it.

I never let my kids see me without a hat or bandanna or wig. I never let anyone take pictures of me with no hair. I didn't need that reminder. I know it was something I went through, but I don't care to ever see that again. Just to remember it now is just too hard.

Chapter 9

Wednesday, July 31, 2002. One day after the hair completely left my head. One day before my second chemo treatment. I was getting a bit nervous. Sure I had had one already, maybe that was why I was more nervous this time.
I knew what to expect. How I would feel. But then I wondered if I would feel worse because it WAS the second one. I just didn't know. I told work that I would be back again as soon as I felt like it. I couldn't give them a timetable for the unknown.

There was a lot on my calendar for the next week. School registrations were starting too. I needed to feel good to be able to register the kids and get them ready for school. After the summer they had, I could only imagine how they must have wanted to return to school.

I was still trying to adjust to the hair 'thing'. I still hadn't looked. I just couldn't bring myself to do it. I meant it when I said no pictures. Why in the world would anyone want to see such an ugly thing? Ick. Because that is how I felt. Incredibly ugly. I really didn't even want any taken of me in the wig.

Thursday came. I had to have my next fill at the plastic surgeon. It hurt this time. This time the fill pushed on my port a little bit so when I went over to the cancer center and they put the needle in to get blood, it hurt a lot. They gave me some numbing medicine for the next two times to put on before I came to chemo so it wouldn't hurt.

I got my blood work done. They said it was wonderful. I thought a couple of things were on the low side, but hemoglobin and platelets were good. (Did I ever expect to have to worry about such things or even know about them? Not ever.) I was told that some people actually start growing hair back during treatment. You don't know how much I wanted to be one of those people, although I knew most likely I wouldn't be. I was told it would probably come back a totally different color. And it could be curly. This makes me think of what I thought of many times at that time. Be careful what you wish for! I always wanted a vacation from work, a breast reduction, and curly hair. I just forgot to specify that I didn't want to get them THIS way!

After the second treatment, I felt a little less 'yucky.' I took one less Decadron than before as it had made me so lightheaded. Maybe that was part of it. The thing I noticed though, is I was much more tired. I had no energy.

Kayla had been crying the night of my second treatment. This poor young soul who was only 10 years old-my heart ached for her. She told me that sometimes she cried because she wondered why I had to go through this. That was two of us. But I tried to reassure her and not dwell on it myself. It was now a fact of my life and I had to deal with it. It was just that sometimes when you see what your body is going through, the port hurts, you see no hair, you can't do what you used to, well then it can get rough.

One day at a time sometimes is a long way to go.

Chapter 10

Sunday, August 4, 2002. I was in pain. Everything hurt. I was more tired than I could ever imagine being. I felt crappy. It was turning out to be a very long day. This was harder than I had ever ever ever imagined it would be. There were many days still that I couldn't believe I had to go through this. I would look at others who were worse off than me and wonder why I thought I had the right to complain. Then I would look at my kids and feel so guilty because where did I have the right to rob them of a normal life for not only the summer but for all of the time to follow.

I would look around the house and become so frustrated. I wanted to be able to clean it, to do what needed to be done by myself without asking for help from anyone. I wanted to be my old self again. I wanted to feel better. I wanted all of it behind me. I wondered at times where that brave strong woman was that everyone was telling me I was. Sometimes it was hard to play that part. Sometimes I did feel sorry for myself. Sometimes I went into the bathroom where no

one could see me or hear me and cried, sobbed.
Where was that brave woman? Sometimes she
took the day off, sometimes she was just tired,
sometimes she went into hiding.

It was the Monday following the second
treatment and I stayed home. I was just too tired
still to try to work. My head hurt and my bones
ached. I didn't expect to be feeling perfect
yet, as I remembered it took a good week to
week and a half to feel back to par after the first
treatment.

Tuesday was registration for the kids. (I still
didn't go to work-I got tired just walking out
to the mailbox for the paper.) I did feel a little
better, so that was a plus. Still had a case of
what I called 'beer head'. If you ever have had
too much beer and got that awful headache
and yucky feeling, you know just what I mean!
It was funny going to registration and getting
compliments on my 'haircut' by people who
didn't know what I was going through. They
would say, "OH you got your haircut." I would
say "Yes something like that." Because I DID get it
cut, although it was all cut off.

Wednesday I went back to work. It was
rough. A couple of hours was more than enough.
I was trying to keep a positive attitude. Yes I
complained sometimes about how I felt and all

of the obvious changes. Who wouldn't? But I was also very thankful that things turned out like they did. That there was no cancer found anywhere else. I knew that many times in the future it would be tough with fears of reoccurrence and appointments for checkups. I just had to hope and pray that this was all of it that God had in store for me. I hoped I was handling it all in the right way and that someday it would be my turn to help others through this. I couldn't help but think that is how in the past I dealt with all the adversities handed to me. I was told once when I was young that I would probably grow up to be a teacher. Who knew it would be in this way?

Thursday it was back to the plastic surgeon for another fill. I didn't know how he managed to keep stretching the expanders and the muscle but he did. And sometimes it just hurt. I was uncomfortable a lot of the time and hoped that the permanent ones wouldn't be that uncomfortable. Sometime after treatment when my blood counts went back up to normal I would have another surgery, this one to put the permanent implants in. Another stinking surgery. I didn't like the thought of that, but it would be nice to have yet another part of all of this behind me. When I was driving to my appointment that day for some reason I got very weepy. It just hit me again of all the appointments I had to keep and the reason for them.

By Friday I was feeling much better. I was no longer tired from my last treatment. It had taken a week this time to get back on my feet. The expanders, on the other hand, still hurt. I felt stretched to the limit. I was very sore.

I have to tell you a bit about the hair at this time. I was not completely bald. It didn't all fall out. You know the people you see portrayed on tv where their hair is partly there? That would pretty much be me. I got another compliment on my haircut. I had thought that the next time someone told me that I should do what one nurse in the hospital told me she did. She took off her wig and handed to the lady. She made her cry though. But see, what struck me was the confidence to do that. I would never have that much!

Speaking of the hair, or lack of it, I finally looked. It was Saturday, August 10th, 2002. I finally looked in the mirror. It didn't hurt THAT much to look. But I thought I looked ugly. At least I never lost my eyelashes or eyebrows like so many do. I was thankful for that little bit. I wanted this to all be over so I could grow hair again. That day looking in the mirror that day felt like a lifetime away.

Chapter 11

Tuesday, August 13, 2002. It had been a busy day. Work, more school registrations, band practice for Kayla, a meeting. I was ready to kick my shoes off and put up my feet. I was feeling great! I always liked this week. The one in between, the one when I felt the best.

On my mind was yet another thing that all this brought about. Not the physical or emotional part of it all, but the financial. Can you imagine how hard it was to make ends meet? Not being able to work really hurt us. The medical bills had started to arrive and even with Tom's good insurance, there was still plenty to pay. Then we had school registrations for four kids, along with school clothes and school supplies. And groceries? I couldn't even buy those. Here I was a mother of four, a caretaker and how do you think that felt? I felt very very inadequate. I was so tired of worrying about how things were going to get paid. I hated it so much. It would be a long time until I could work the hours that I needed to. I had another treatment coming up and would be off of work again for a few days, just in time to not be able to pay for school lunch tickets. I had to forego a couple of bills just to be able to afford shoes for the kids. It was something that bothered me a lot. When I woke up at night I would think about it and not be able to sleep. I never knew that day that the doctor called and said "I have some tough news for you" that SO many aspects of my life would be changed. Virtually everything.

I had yet another appointment at the plastic surgeon for another fill. He had asked how I was doing and I told him I was having a bad week. He just laughed and said he was glad that he wasn't the only one and I had made his day! This time there was no room to stretch me anymore. That made me happy. I couldn't go the next week because I was having treatment number three on Wednesday and Thursday I knew I would not be getting out of my chair. I would come back in two weeks and if I was still the same, I would possible be done with the fills.

Saturday, August 17,2002 was a good day. Strike that. It was a GREAT day. The weather was gorgeous. I felt great. I was in a good mood. I had my rock and roll blaring, the windows open and there was a wonderful breeze coming through the house. I loved it. I told my kids, and I still do, that I will be 80 years old driving down the road in my car with my jeans and t-shirt and I'll be rocking out to the radio. Can't you just picture it?

Wednesday, August 21, 2002. Treatment number three. Tough as always. The lab tech told me that people told her they get sick to their stomach just driving by the cancer center. My stomach was turning and my eyes tearing as I drove there. I knew it was because I had to think of why I was driving there. That was something I could not escape.

They did my lab, weigh in, and yes, every time I gained a little bit thanks to the chemo..... I didn't like it at all. They took my blood pressure which considering the circumstance, was great. They did the usual blood work. I then sat in my little room forever for my follow up before my treatment. Why do they make you wait so long? Too much time to sit there and think. I had to hear about how my 'aggressive treatment' because of the size of my tumor, its aggressiveness and my age. That meant 6 weeks of radiation treatment after this and then drug therapy. This was another of those slap in my face moments. I hated this so much. I hated it happened to me. I used to wonder about my old age and if I would get the dreaded CANCER. I never ever dreamed I would be dealing with this beast at age 44. It just didn't seem quite fair.

I didn't want to deal with this anymore. I was tired of all of it. Please God, I just wanted to wake up from this nightmare.

Chapter 12

Friday, August 23, 2002. I was feeling pretty crappy as expected. I was napping, but not enough. This time everything smelled bad to me and nothing to eat sounded good.

I was alone as the kids were back in school and Tom was working. I had a couple of those moments again. When you are sitting home alone, feeling like I was for the reason I was that should come as no surprise. What the trigger was this time, did surprise me. I was watching a show about babies being born and I totally lost it. It made me long for that time in my life so long ago. Back when I had a life just like everyone else and the biggest worry was whose turn it was to change the diaper or feed the baby. The lack of sleep from those days was from a wonderful blessing-not from the treatment of a life threatening disease.

The 'yuckies' seemed to be hanging on longer this time. I was so ready for it to be past. Not just for this time but completely. I still wasn't sleeping. I would wake up and worry. About everything from my health to my finances. I would hear the doctors words often still creeping into my mind. "I have some tough news." Would I ever forget them? I had a hunch I wouldn't.

Tuesday I pulled myself up and hauled myself out and back to work. I really wasn't up to par but didn't want to sit at home moping another day, thinking of the things that scared me.

I had a question for my family and friends at this time. So I asked them. I had been thinking as usual. Missing the old days, the old me. Realizing that everything would be different from then on, but for the first time, hoping that didn't mean it was going to be all bad. It seemed at the time that it was going to be a long time until this was all behind me. But then it would never be behind me, what with a lifetime of checkups before me. So I got to wondering while I was thinking, how people, family, friends, 'saw' me now.

Did they see me as the one who simply is undergoing treatment ,had cancer, lost her hair....or did anyone see me as I was/I am? You know, the same old me. I wanted to know. I got such amazing responses. Most made me cry. No one did see me as a cancer patient. My brother posted a picture he made up to explain. It was funny and touching at the same time. He put my head on the body of Wonder Woman.

I loved it but at the same time, felt the pressure. Sometimes I didn't feel I was that super woman that everyone thought I was or saw. Sometimes when I was alone, I felt very weak, inadequate. I often wondered how much of this I could really take. There were moments that I wondered just how long I could last. Was there really going to be an end of the road for this? Could I really do it all? Then I would look at my kids and my strength would return. I knew I would do whatever it took to be well and be there for them. I knew what it was like to grow up without one of your parents. I had no intentions of letting them know that kind of pain.

Chapter 13

Thursday, August 29,2002. Another milestone in this journey was done. At least I thought so at the time. I had the last 'fill' at the plastic surgeons. I wouldn't have to go back until all my treatments were done. Then two months after radiation I was to have surgery to have the 'switch.' I would have the expanders taken out and the permanent implants put in. It seemed like so far away at the time. And I did not like the idea of yet another surgery, of course, but the idea of getting the expanders out was inviting. They were always uncomfortable. I was also hoping that the 'new' ones would at least help me look and feel more normal. Maybe I wouldn't feel like the Bride of Frankenstein anymore. If you could see the scars, you would understand that statement. They put them on the bottom to try to hide them the best they can, but to this day , every day I see them, every day the reminder of what I went through is right before me in the mirror. I could almost forget until I get a glimpse of me in the mirror and there the permanent reminder is and will always be.

About this time I posed another question to the readers of my online journal. (Hey I couldn't help it, I had always been a thinker in my life and should have probably been a philosophy major!) I asked them. "When you think of me and this crap (well it was) or when you talk about it do you say/think that I HAVE or HAD breast cancer?? For me I always thought in the tense HAD. I felt the surgery took the tumor. The lymph nodes were clear and all subsequent tests were negative. I was glad to see that all answers were the same. Everyone said HAD! I liked the past tense.

September arrived as it does each fall. I worked on Labor Day like I always did while the rest of the family had a day off. I managed to catch a cold. I worried about being able to have my last treatment. I was on the countdown to the very last time I had to endure chemo and there was nothing I wanted to stop it. A cold could. It could mess with my blood counts and if they were too low I would have to postpone the last one.

September 3,2002. Just 9 days to go until the last treatment. Still had a bit of a cold but I was feeling better. I started to think of what the last one meant. I wouldn't have to feel icky again, but best of all-HAIR!! I could not imagine having hair again. Kind of ironic isn't it? A few short months earlier , I could not imagine NOT having hair. I would look in the mirror and it was all so surreal. I would see me looking back. But how could that be me?

Jamie was looking at me funny that night. I had on just a bandanna, like I did when I was home. He tried to peek around the back of it. I just told him, Yes, Jamie mom has no hair. Well, not much of it anyway. That seemed to be enough for him. I was glad.

You know it is so funny how some things just 'happen' to cheer you or whatever just at the 'right' moment. (There are no coincidences, right?) I hadn't been extremely down about things, I was just impatient to have everything done. I was fighting with the image of the new me or the me at the moment with how I felt I should look or be. I was trying to grasp how I could have had cancer and never even feel sick. I had never smoked, rarely drank anything, thought I lived a healthy life. It was hard to see young women or even older women for that matter on tv or anywhere that looked good, had their hair and all their 'woman parts.'

I went to get the mail that day and I received a wonderful card from a friend of my mom's that I had known my whole life. It simply said, "May your prayers be answered." I know I had been

praying a lot. I knew they were being answered.
As a matter of fact, the day I was going to go
into surgery, when I was sitting at the table, so
quiet, I was thinking if I only knew it would all
be okay, I knew I could get through this. In that
moment, a piece of paper fell a little bit out of
the container I kept my bills in. On one side was
address labels. On the other, the side I could see?
Simply two words. ANSWERED PRAYERS! That was
the moment I was sure I would be fine. And I still
have that piece of paper yet today.

I also had a package in the mail. I open it up
and inside was a wonderful bear with wings.
It said Wings across its chest. It also had wings on
its feet-one with a halo, the other a pink ribbon.
The little card hooked to the bear said "WINGS
Holy Bear-Women Involved in Nurturing, Giving,
Sharing. To honor all those whose lives have been
touched by breast cancer." On the other page
it said. "For I know the plans I have for you
declares the LORD-plans to give you hope and
a future." WOW. Hope and a future. That teared
me right up. I wanted to carry it everywhere
it was so great. I did add it to my growing
collection of angels and bears.

The third thing in the mail that day was a
book called, "No More Bad Hair Days" by a
woman who had cancer and just wrote down
her thoughts. I could relate to so many. Humor

is so important when you go through something like this! (I later passed this book onto my cousin when she was going through breast cancer treatment too-for the second time in her 47 years!)

The next week, Daniel came home from school with a sack and handed it to me. One of his teachers makes baskets. He had asked her to make one for me when he told her about me! She handed him the basket and said "No charge" People just continued to be so generous and so giving. I cannot tell you how many times. I can say I was a very lucky person. I felt truly blessed.

Tuesday, September 12, 2002. Was it time? Would this really be my last chemo treatment? Back in June and July and even August of that year, this day had seemed so far away. And now here it was. I was looking forward to walking out of there and not looking back. I wanted this part of the journey over so badly. I had been told by those going through it, that when they were done, they were sad, even scared, because although while going through it, it could be horrible, at least you knew you were actively fighting it. I wondered if I would feel the same. I had a hunch I wouldn't. I thought I might even leave the cancer center singing! I felt fine. I was fine. Chemo made me feel crappy. I knew it was done for a purpose but I was ready to be done and move on, to get on with my life. I still had radiation to look forward to. But now, I hated looking at myself. It was ugly. It was a reminder all the time of all I had been through and was going through. I could not wait for it to grow back. I even vowed I would never again complain about shaving!

I dreaded this day as much as relished that it was here. I dreaded the familiar smells and I knew how hard it would be driving there.

I managed to get there fine and the smells DID bother me immensely. I had to hold my nose a lot. But I made it through. And I DIDN'T feel let down at all when I walked out of there. I was done. Dear God, I was done! I had so much to look forward to. In a month that pesky port would come out. My hair would grow back. My last course of treatment, radiation would be starting. And MY HAIR WOULD GROW BACK!

Someone sent me a saying at this time that fit so much and I think of it often. "If God brings you to it....God will bring you through it."

Chapter 14

It was the next day after my last treatment. They yuckies were mild so far. Better than the last time at least. I was tired as I was waking up very early and was not able to go back to sleep.

I found out that my port would come out on October 10th. It would be done in the surgeon's office and not in the hospital. I didn't even know that they did things like that in the office. But I was glad I didn't have to make another trip to the hospital. It was supposed to take 45 minutes and then I would be done. Something to look forward to.

By Sunday things had changed. I had a rough day. It surprised me because the day before I had felt really good. Sunday made up for it. Every part of me ached. It hurt to be touched anywhere. I was more tired than usual. And I developed that metal taste in my mouth that can come with having chemo. There was no relieving it. And the smells? They were all bad, bad, bad! I vowed I would make it through that week. I had to keep looking forward, past this to when I would feel better.

I had been looking around that day at my family and the pictures of everyone and got to thinking about all of them. I thought about how this all had changed not only me but others too. But I was not the same. By no choice of my own. It just boggled me for a moment that day again that this had even happened to me. Never ever before this in my mind did I think anything like this could possibly happen to me. I tried to stay away from the why of it all. I sometimes wondered about the how. What caused it? I guess you could drive yourself crazy thinking about it all. I tried to just look ahead, tried to feel better. I posted a request this day in my journal. I knew people were praying for me and my recovery, but I asked them to pray that this never came back again.

By Wednesday I was feeling better. Not one hundred percent, but better. Every day was a little better and I would take that, especially knowing since I would never have to do this again. The thought of feeling better excited me! I couldn't wait to be able to tackle closets and bedrooms. I was thrilled at the moment to be able to do dishes again. It felt great to do some of the everyday stuff that we normally complain about. I was looking forward to the day when I could go outside without any hair coverage.

I couldn't wait to put my face up to the sun and let the wind blow my own little hairs around. Just to be able to go outside and not hang on to the top of my head so the wig didn't take off in the wind was a pleasing prospect.

Everywhere I went or everything I watched or everything I read seemed all about breast cancer. It was everywhere. I couldn't escape it. There was stories, and statistics, some happy endings, some not. I didn't want to be bombarded by it. Sometimes it was just more than I could bear.

Sunday, September 22,2002. Kayla and I did something that we had not been able to do for almost 3 months. We spent the day out together, just mother and daughter! It was fabulous. We spent the rest of the afternoon 'doing art.' I matted a sketch I had done and hung it up. First time I had ever done that. It turned out quite good too. And it still hangs on my wall to this day. It was good doing something creative. It was better sharing the time with my daughter.

Monday was a different story. I thought this emotional roller coaster would have ended long ago. I didn't realize at the time it was a lifetime ride. I had one of those moments again. They were becoming further apart, but once in awhile reality would hit. I was in taking my hair off so I could cook-it was synthetic so it could melt just taking something out of the oven. I had gotten another look at myself again. I hated it so much. I felt so ugly and deformed. I cannot explain it to those of you who haven't been through it. But believe me, it so bites. The old me was gone. I couldn't seem to put that behind me yet. For good or bad, that person no longer existed. Maybe it would have been easier if I hadn't liked the old me, but I liked that person I was just fine, thank you. Some days I needed just to grieve for that person who was now gone. I thought that the next year when all the operations were done and behind me and when the hair had grown back and things got back to 'normal' that then it would be easier. I knew I would never be completely at ease for there would always be the tests. The tests to check. For cancer. To see if it had come back. Always the tests. I prayed and still do every day that it doesn't come back. I don't want to ever have to handle this situation again.

Chapter 15

Thursday September 26,2002. My radiation consult. It was another of those reality visits, a real wake up, a revisit to my nightmare. It was very rough listening to all that he had to say. Especially alone. I had no one that went with me to hold my hand this time. I had wished I had. I hadn't expected it to be as bad as the first one I had to endure with my other doctor. Tom was there holding my hand then. I had wished he was here now.

The doctor was very nice and considerate. He spoke in terms that anyone could understand. I thought at least the people there would make my 7 and ½ weeks of going in better. Yes you heard it. SEVEN AND A HALF WEEKS of radiation! 36 times. Thirty-six. He told me if I did nothing from this point on, considering the large tumor and close margins, even though everything was negative, my chances for reoccurrence were at LEAST 50% and as high as 90%. Dear God. That was so hard having to hear that. I wondered if he was sure he was talking about ME! He said the 'good' thing is, with this radiation, it reduced the chance to almost nothing. I had a 'potentially curable' tumor. His words. I wasn't sure I even liked those.

I would start in about 10 days. He wanted me to be a little further from chemo but still in the 4 week time frame I had to be in to start radiation. Remember I thought I was done with fills at the plastic surgeon? Nope. The next week I had to actually go back to have some taken out of one of the expanders. If I didn't it would get in the way of the rays. Could I not do anything normally? It seemed to always be something!

I had to be weighed and the chemo had put 20 pounds back on. I was none too happy. I was told that was common from the stuff I had and the drugs they give you, but to keep eating good for it was important for cell regeneration.

I was told the only probable side effects to radiation would be possible fatigue and of course, the burning of the skin. Goody. They would give me cream for the skin.

They would not only be radiating the area where the tumor was but also the lymph nodes even though they were negative. It was hard getting used to the fact that I would have to be spending every day for 7 and ½ weeks getting radiation. I knew it was the down side of the mountain, or at least I hoped so. There was still so much ahead.

Around this same time, my cousin , the one I mentioned earlier had also gotten a diagnosis of breast cancer. She had underwent a biopsy and then they had told her that they did not think it was cancer. Well, it didn't turn out that way at all. The final report was cancer. But his was her second time fighting it. Her mom had to fight it twice and now she had to too. She first was diagnosed when she was only 29. Here it was 17 years later and she was going to have to go through it all again. I just could not imagine.

I hated this disease with a passion. I hated that anyone had to go through it. I was tired of hearing about it everywhere. It seemed it was on the news every night. It was like it would never go away. I felt like I was being bombarded. I realized that peace of mind was now a thing of the past.

October 1, 2002. I had one of those laugh out loud I can't believe I did this times. Those of us who have been through this blame it on chemo brain. You know all those cells it kills? We insist it takes a few brain cells too.

I had accidentally thrown my wig in with the wash. I must have picked it up with the laundry in my room. I didn't know it until I went to put the laundry in the dryer and there it was. Oh dear!

Luckily it didn't melt. I could even wear it shortly after that-spin dry is great. And oh, it smelled so Mountain Fresh!

October every year is breast cancer awareness month. I knew we would be bombarded even more on the news, in the paper, everywhere. I was right. The local paper ran a big ad on the 1st. It was a reminder to get a mammogram-that was okay-so that you weren't a STATISTIC. Excuse me but I am NOT a statistic. I thought I was a person. It did not sit well with me, so I wrote the following letter to the editor and sent it.

Cancer Can Strike Anyone

It's been on the news everywhere these days: stories of breast cancer and sometimes even about those it affects.

In your paper on Monday was a large ad talking about how over 200,000 women would be diagnosed in 2002 with breast cancer. It urged women to get a mammogram so they wouldn't be a statistic.

As one of those 200,000 women, I would like to point out that I am not a statistic. I am a wife, a mother, a person with a job and someone who had a normal life before this diagnosis. I want every woman to know or be aware that this can happen to anyone. I had no family history of breast cancer, no known risk factors, no reason to get this. It was a combination of things that led me to find it. From a shooting pain, that led to self exam to then a mammogram and ultrasound. If I listened to the news about all the tests and how they may not be effective imagine how different things would be today.

I urge all women to be aware of their body and any changes. Trust your instinct as I did. Believe in the old adage, better safe than sorry. Do those self exams and the yearly mammograms. And never believe it can't happen to you. It can. It does. I am living proof.

Chapter 16

Thursday, October 3,2002. That was one day I was glad was over. I started the day very early with a visit to the plastic surgeon. He took about 160cc of saline out of the left expander. We didn't know if that was enough at the time, we had to wait for the results of all the scans and everything that I would go through that day. Yes more scans. I did find out from him that day if all went well, I would have the operation to switch to permanent implants on Dec 30th. I prayed all went well. I could be a whole new me for the new year!

That afternoon was my radiation planning session. You just have no clue until you go through something like this what it all entails. My poor arm was asleep by the time they were done measuring, marking, x-raying, and tattooing. Yes I said tattooing. They had to put small dots-actual tattoos for the radiologists to use to line everything up perfectly for the radiation beams. You cannot be off at all. My arm went to sleep during this since I had to hold it up so long and the therapist had to lower it down for m.

After that it was off to the waiting room for another CT scan and x-rays of the spot where the tumor had been. It was done just for the planning. But I couldn't help but be very nervous in the waiting room waiting to get it done. The mind kept thinking, what if there IS something there this time????? I swallowed hard. Told myself NO, don't think that way.

Finally I was called to the CT room and had to put the arms up again. This time they moved me around to where I had to be and told me not to move. My jaw even locked up during this. I finally got done there and my arm felt like rubber.

I must tell you. You almost have to have an out of body experience to get through all this. I felt that way many times through the whole ordeal. It often felt like I was an observer for all of this. I think that was an easier way to cope than actually feeling it all at the time. I had a thought. I was thinking how the bodies we have aren't really ours anyway. We use them for however long we have them. But our souls. That is different. Our souls are ours alone. And that , my friend is something they could not touch or change or take away by any of their medicines, procedures or operations.

Friday I got a call about when radiation treatments would start. ALL tests came back good. We were ready to go. Originally it was going to start on the next Thursday but they moved it up one day to Wednesday. I did the counting on the calendar and this was too good to be true. If all went well, and I didn't get sick and the weather cooperated the whole time the 36th day, the day I would finish would be the very day before Thanksgiving! A sweeter irony, I don't think there ever was.

Wednesday, October 9,2002. Only 35 more radiation treatments to go! It was a lot easier and quicker than I thought it would be. It only takes a matter of minutes once you are changed and called back. The worst part of it I thought would be the inconvenience, having to take the time out of each and every day to go have it done.

Once a week during radiation you had to have a doctor's visit. They did the usual of weighing you, taking blood, checking the radiated site. I also had to have 'pictures' taken too to make sure everything is going okay and they don't have to change any of their variables.

After the first visit, I stopped at the Mercy Breast Health Center to visit with the nurse case manager, Shari. I told you just a little about this earlier. To say our area is very lucky to have such a program is an understatement. Shari is one of the most empathetic understanding people you could ever meet. The perfect pick for a difficult job. One I would never want. She is the one that is with the person from when they first visit the doctor after finding out their 'tough news' to the hospital, to chemo, and aftercare. I was one who was definitely grateful for such a program.

The next day on Thursday, I had to go to the surgeon's office to get that annoying port out. I went alone again. Seemed the more I got into all of this, that I was pretty much going alone to everything. I don't know if my family thought I didn't need anyone with me anymore or what. But guess what? Some of those days sitting there alone in the waiting rooms, I longed for that hand to hold. I knew this cancer thing was truly a journey I had to endure, but still, to have the support was really important. Because it was always frightening.

They had a room for office surgery that I went into. I had already formed a lot of scar tissue in that small amount of time. They had to cauterize to get off the scar tissue. It was so surreal once again to be laying there as the doctor was burning that off. I could see the smoke and smell the burning flesh. Thank goodness I could not feel it, although whatever they gave me to numb the area made up for it as that was extremely painful. I did feel him do a few stitches but that was no big deal. The soreness started soon after I left so I took something for it and went about my business. I couldn't help but think another step was done along this journey. Now what was a good hair growing chant?!

Chapter 17

Friday, October 11,2002. Three treatments down, 33 to go! Every time I went it seemed as it I was just there. But then I would lay there while they did all their adjustments, and during the treatment, thinking of lots of strange things. One thing that I couldn't escape from was why I was even there in the first place. Not that I ever forgot, that would be impossible. But some days, almost..

I got to thinking on this day that how this stuff that was supposed to help me-that could make me 'potentially cured' could also do a lot of harm. Of course because its radiation, everyone has to leave the room but you. You can't be pregnant obviously. It would probably burn the skin before I was all through. And the worse thing? It could even cause the very disease it was trying to prevent.

I was still waiting for the first signs of fuzz on my head and getting very impatient. Chemotherapy had been done for a month, it was time for that stuff to get growing.

The port site remained very sore. More so than when it was put in. I was getting very tired of all the pain and aches I was constantly feeling.

Tuesday October 15, 2002. It was doctor day at the cancer center. Every Tuesday after my treatment I would have to visit the doctor so he could check out things, including to see if I was getting burned. It was a sobering thing to have the doctor come in with a huge three ring binder and know it was all about you. How in the world did I go from never ever having anything wrong, from being very healthy, to this????????

On this day everything looked good, including the skin. But it was early in this part of the journey yet. I felt good, too. Going strong as he put it. Absolutely I was. That was the kicker in all of it too. The ONLY time I had felt crappy or sick or slightly bad was during chemo. I felt like myself all of the time other than that. Wouldn't you think when we had all that awful 'other stuff' , cancer, how I hate saying that word- almost like saying it gives it strength, that we should at least feel sick. Shouldn't we feel when something has gone wrong inside us?

Wednesday. Six down and 30 to go. I was looking forward to the next day when I could say only 29 to go. Each day was one day closer to being done and 29 left sounded way better to me than 30 did. This day the lady who was called ahead of me got finished with her treatment. I was happy for her, but couldn't help but feel a little bit jealous. It was one of those days that felt like I was going to be coming back every day forever. When you got finished with all your treatments they gave you a certificate of completion. Whoopee. Now I am sure it is with all great intentions. But a certificate of completion? I would be sure to just run right out and get a frame to put that up on the wall to always remind me of what I just went through. Only not. Hey but if I did, I could put it right next to the Welcome Letter I got from the Cancer Center at the beginning of all this. Yes, I forgot to tell you about that one. I actually got a letter welcoming me to the Cancer Center. That was one welcome I could have lived without in my life!

Thursday, October 17, 2002. Lying there this day, I got to thinking. Yes, again. ONLY 7 down. Felt like 17. Felt like 70. Was that all that I had been there? SEVEN times? Every day it was all too familiar. And I had to go back 29 more times. That day it felt like 290. I was never going to be done with this nightmare. I was sure of it.

Chapter 18

Friday, October 18, 2002. It was Friday. I was free for two whole days. I didn't have to do anything I didn't want to. No appointments, nothing. It was a wonderful feeling. And so was my fuzzy head!!! Yes! It was finally growing back. Fuzz glorious fuzz. The small glimmer of hair, hope. I would have hair again. I was ecstatic! They had told me it would take 6-8 weeks for the hair to start coming back. Here I was at 5 weeks out and mine was starting to return. It meant of course, the hair would return on my legs and underarms too. I hadn't missed having to shave at all! I told them at rads that day that they would need to let me know when the underarm hair was getting too long for them. They told me not to worry, they have scissors! Tom wanted to see my new fuzz and at work they threatened to take the wig off to see it. I don't think so! Not so soon. It was only a little fuzz that was just starting to grow but I was very happy.

That light at the end of the tunnel was suddenly a big brighter! I went and got out my box of cards to reread. During all this time, from the moment I was diagnosed through treatment, each day I would go to the mailbox and there would be many cards to cheer me. Some made me cry! My sister bought me a box to put them all in and I still have that box full of cards to this day. I know I will keep them forever. I love taking them out and reading them, even when they do make me cry, because that is a good cry.

I got a call this Friday afternoon from the middle school. My youngest son almost choked to death on a sandwich. There was a sub there that did the Heimlich on him. He had to get her attention by pointing at his throat. He didn't know this sub so I could not thank her. It was very scary for him as you can imagine. (He was actually the second one to do that. My oldest when he was in middle school choked on a cinnamon roll. A guidance counselor helped him. He almost couldn't get it to come out. Even he was scared! I DID thank him and when I see him to this day, I think about how he saved my son.) You may wonder why I put this in a story on breast cancer. Well it is a reminder that no matter what was happening to me, life went on as usual. Stuff did happen to other people. It wasn't all about me by far. Oh and if you are wondering, I did tell Kayla when she got to middle school, make sure that she chewed her food good. So far so good!

Sunday, October 20,2002. It was one of those days again. Maybe it was the dreary weather contributing to it, who knows? I refused to go on my online journal and sugarcoat it this day. Didn't feel like saying, Hi all, everything is great. I am fine and blah blah blah. Sometimes you just didn't feel that way and sometimes I just wanted to have those feelings that weren't so great and fine and wonderful. Human nature, I suppose. Then I would worry about worrying. What about the stress that caused? What about the stress of everyday living? Could all that stressing cause me harm? Did it cause all this in the first place? I could drive myself crazy! I just wanted to find a place to let out one great big primal scream. Then maybe I would feel better.

The next day of course was Monday. I had lots of things going on. A Monday at work. A recheck on my incision where the port was removed, and of course another trip to get radiated. (My son often joked I was going to start glowing in the dark!) And it was x-ray day also. I had a meeting at the high school with Jamie's 'regular' teachers on how they graded Jamie. Why I really needed to go and hear that I don't know. Write me a memo! Sometimes I think they just like to call meetings for the fun of it.

Tuesday I got home later than I thought I would. It was doctor day once again. Hurry and wait I call it. For what? They checked my skin. It was a little red. Then I had to go get a blood test. Routine. Maybe for them. But I felt then and I still do that for me, they are far from routine. I got nervous at every test they put me through. At every picture they would take. I still do. I hate having to live this way.

When I went to have this test, the waiting room was full. I wondered if there was that much more cancer out there or was I just noticing it more? It seemed to me it was all I heard about. Or about people dying from it more. Some days I wanted to be an ostrich and put my head in the sand just so I didn't have to hear any of it. Don't get me wrong, my positive attitude remained. It is just so unbelievable sometimes where we find ourselves.

Wednesday, October 23, 2002. 11 down. 25 to go. Was it going fast enough? I didn't know. It was so automatic by then, I would just go when it was time, get changed, wait, be radiated, change back, go about my day. And do it all over again the next day. This week they had taken x-rays every day. They must have had the beam off by just a little bit. I was hoping they got it right again finally, I was getting tired of the constant x-rays.

The waiting room on this day was literally standing room only. I remained the youngest one there. By far. It made me feel conspicuous. I wondered if they were wondering why I was there. Or feeling sorry for me since I was so young. I myself felt sorry for every one of us there for having to go through what we did.

By this time my skin was starting to get red and be a little sore. I couldn't imagine what it would be like by the time I had 25 more radiation treatments.

Thursday I was home because one of the kids was sick. I took some time to look back at what I had been through. I could not believe I had been without hair for three months! I let the kids get a glimpse of it growing back. They told me it was 'gross.' I said no it is not gross, it is GREAT! It was coming back now...and coming back dark from what I could tell. Gross was when it was coming out. I figured, though, it would still be a long time before it was of any decent length.

After Thursday's appointment I was one-third of the way done with radiation. Every day I went it seemed as if I had been there forever. With forever to go. But each day I walked out of there knowing it was one less time that I had to go it. That I was thankful for!

Friday, October 25, 2002. I was glad it was Friday and I would have those two days away. I spent some time on a Breast Cancer Survivor board. Normally it was a great place to go for support and understanding for all the people on there had been there because they had all had breast cancer too. This visit we had had a board guest host. She posed a question that surprised and shocked quite a few of us. She wanted to know if we would rather die of cancer or old age?! HELLO?! Did she actually expect that there would be one of us that would choose cancer?! Dying at any age of course could be unpleasant, obviously and this is what she was getting at with old age. BUT! Why would she ask that question to a bunch of young women who worried about dying too young and leaving our kids behind? Who worried about not seeing their kids grow up, graduate, marry, or have kids of their own? At least if you died of old age you could say that you lived your life and saw what you wanted to see. Do you suppose any of our relatives who left us at an early age would have chosen that? And how or why could she ever think that dying of cancer would be any less difficult? From what I have seen when my loved ones were dying from cancer, it was difficult. For everyone. And when I thought it could be me, there were no words in the English Language to describe the anguish that that brought to me. Thanks, but I still choose old age.

Chapter 19

Sunday October 27, 2002. You would think I would learn the first time. After that bit on the breast cancer support board-you know the 'do you want to die of old age or cancer' horrible question bit-you would think I would have stayed away. But no. I wouldn't listen to anyone. I had to go back. I had made friends there. And back I went. The discussion this time came from a poster on the boards. She insisted a doctor should never tell you that you are cured, for there is NO cure from cancer. And most likely after you have it once, it WILL come back. Wow. Talk about trying to take the wind out of your sails! I choose to look at things a little differently than her. I try to always remain positive. What is the point otherwise? Don't get me wrong, many days that is not easy, especially when I read of so many dying from breast cancer. I hate seeing that. Some of them have battled it for years, some got a different cancer and died and they still said it was from breast cancer. Which I could never figure out why because if they were free of this beast and it came back as another different cancer maybe one didn't have anything to do with the other. Anyhow, it is always hard to read something like that. I wished many times I could turn the old hands of time back and this had never happened to me.

Monday. 22 more to go. It seemed this day to be going very fast. My skin looked good. It wasn't even pink. I guess it helped to have the weekend off.

Monday was just a busy regular life day. I loved those. I think I ran ten minutes behind all day. We had dentist appointments, Kayla had a concert. When I said that was it for the day, Kayla said, "But mom, you forgot to schedule relax!" What a sweetie. I told her I would get to do that when I got home. I loved being busy. It sure beat the alternative and it was wayyyyy better than just sitting in my recliner.

Kayla's concert was great and I actually enjoyed going to it. Because I could. Understand, many parents complain about going to these concerts, not me. I remember when I went to her first middle school concert, actually the summer before middle school, there were a few parents there, talking, acting bored. And there was me. Tears rolling down my face. I am sure most wondered why I was sitting at this concert and crying. I was crying because I was sitting at this concert! Period. I was still here and able to be listening to my daughter in her first middle school concert. I relished every single note.

Tuesday-doctor day as usual at the Cancer Center. He said so far, so good. Blood counts and everything from the week before looked good. Whew! I never tired of hearing that! Oh and only 21 more to go.

Wednesday. 20 more to go. I was lying there that day and it was all a bit surreal for some reason. It was strange to have to drop everything no matter where I was and run to the Cancer Center and get radiated. Then I a couple minutes I would be done and on my way until the next time. I was looking forward to that Friday when I could say I was half done and the downside of the countdown would begin. It seemed like I had been dealing with this for a long time by this point and I knew I would be dealing with it forever but not in the everyday way that I was at this point.

I went to that website yet again. Seems I couldn't learn to stay away. There was more on the subject of never being cured. And that you could never say you were. For this cancer is a systemic one, they said, so you could count on getting it again somewhere else. WHAT?! Why does talk like that belong on a breast cancer survivors board? I didn't need to hear that. I wanted to stay positive, to not be scared again.

I wondered if the people saying it had no faith? Well I did. I believed in miracles! I thought well, God can cure can't he? I planned on staying positive and living my life as close to normal as I possibly could.

I watched the kids walk to the bus that day and I got teary-eyed. I could not imagine NOT being there for them. They needed me at this time in their life especially and it choked me up for a moment thinking about the reality of it all. I thought about what their world would be like if I wasn't in it. It was a picture in my mind that I never wanted to become a reality. So while I was home alone, I cried. And then I got angry about all of it once again. I really wanted this emotional roller coaster to stop right then. I was ready to get off of it.

Chapter 20

November. It was Friday November 1st! I was now officially half way done. I was marking the calendar off and the three weeks and three days I had left didn't look like so long. Having to drop everything each day to go get this done sure made things hectic. Sometimes I wasn't done at work and would have to go back there and I had so many other things going on.

While I was there this particular Friday, I heard some man talking about how this was a life-changing experience. That nothing was the same anymore. Nothing. Truer words were never spoken. I agreed nothing was the same anymore nor would it ever be again. Some things become not so important. Other things become very important. This lady said to him, that he was back where he was, though so it should be the same as before. He said no, I will never ever be the same. I sadly knew what he meant!

Saturday came and I was glad. I loved the weekends. I liked them because I felt more normal, I didn't have to feel like a patient. Mondays always seemed to come too fast.

Sunday, November 3, 2002. I had a do nothing kind of day. I just hung out with the family and I loved it. What a nice change that was. My arm was hurting a lot and even still tingling-something that I have found never goes away. I had a couple of 'those moments' that day. Sometimes it was still so very hard and so unbelievable. Next year and even the next week seemed so far away. One day at a time can take a long long time. I wanted to be done and healthy and to never have to do that again. How realistic was that, I wondered, now that I had battled cancer once already. I didn't want to think about it, I couldn't live like that.

Monday it was back for another treatment. 17 left to go. So so many. Time was going fast yet slow. I saw another 'young' person there that day. She had to be in her forties and she was there with her sister. I heard her talking about how they would do both sides of her head this time. I really hated this disease.

Tuesday, November 5, 2002. I had to wait for treatment for a half an hour. I knew it was going to be a little later because the person in front of me had to take longer for some reason. Then it was doctor day. I got called back there right away but got to sit and wait for 30 minutes for him to come in. He was there about 30 seconds. He looked at my skin. It was a little red, mostly under the arm. The nurse told me to walk around with my hand on my hip with a little attitude at home. That was so it didn't rub so much. I told her my family would be constantly looking at me going What? Thinking they did something. The doctor told me my skin looked better than most at this stage. BUT (there is always one of those) since I had 16 more to go, 8 more than most people my skin would most likely be raw by the end of treatment. Goody, something to look forward to. I had to give them a tube of blood-last one during radiation. The tech was great, quick and painless. Which is a trick, because I can now only offer my left arm for blood drawing and IV's. Once you have lymph nodes removed from one side, that is from then on, off limits. And wouldn't you know it, my right side was always the easiest one to find good veins in.

In my journal that day, I posted a saying I had found, the author is anonymous so I want to share it with you. Read the words, and think about them. They are so very true.

What Cancer Cannot Do

Cancer is so limited...

It cannot cripple Love

It cannot shatter Hope

It cannot corrode Faith

It cannot destroy Peace

It cannot kill Friendship

It cannot suppress Memories

It cannot silence Courage

It cannot invade the Soul

It cannot steal eternal Life

It cannot conquer the Spirit.

-author unknown

Chapter 21

Wednesday, November 6, 2002. I was very tired. Emotionally. Physically. Just 15 more treatments to go. There was three new people there that day. That was only the new ones I saw while I was there for such a short time. I couldn't imagine how many there actually were. Wow.

Some days it was still hard to go there, to lay there being a patient, thinking about how fast and easily things in your life can change.

Every part of me hurt that day. I needed to just sit and put my feet up, the let my short little hairs breathe. I couldn't wait to throw away the wig. Especially at the doctors where I would change to be radiated. There was so much static electricity the hairs on the wig would stand straight up.

Thursday I only worked part of the day. My arm couldn't take a full day. It ached so much. It really upset me when I had to go tell the assistant manager I had to go home that my arm hurt too much to input any more orders. I got teary eyed and thought I would cry right then. It was so frustrating. I hated not being able to do my job.

14 treatments to go. Two weeks and three days. Tom came because he got off early, but I was already called back into the room. At least after all this time, he finally saw where I was going every day. I had x-rays taken yet again. My once a week pictures to make sure those rays are going where they want them to and not somewhere else. It's bad enough they will destroy tissue where they are pointing it, I didn't need it harming any more of me than it had to.

Friday. 13 to go. My skin was getting redder by the day. I was glad to have the weekend off to rest it, but knew as soon as Monday came it would quickly become red again. I was talking with one of the techs that day. I told him I liked them all fine and not to take it personal, but I would sure be glad when I didn't have to see their faces every day. He told me that they meet a lot of nice people in this job, but that they wished it was under different circumstances. I understood that!

That morning started a bit rough. I got to the obituary page in the paper. A lady I met a couple months earlier at the support group had died. I was shocked to see it. She was still working at the time I met her and looked good. And yes, this was her second time battling it, it had returned. First breast cancer, then to her liver. It made me very sad and terrified me all at the same time. God, please don't let that ever be me! I could hardly breathe.

That night I hugged my family a little tighter, told them again that I loved them. Something that I had always done, and meant, but that somehow now took on a whole new meaning. You just never knew when it would be too late. I didn't want to have regrets. Life had taken a whole new turn for me, and I was determined to find the good out of all that had happened to me.

Sunday I was driving. And you know when the sun kind of peeks through the clouds and you can see the rays? A few years ago when Kayla was very young, she had said she thought that was God's light shining down on us. She believed it. Now whenever I see those rays, no matter what, no matter where, I think of that. It makes me smile. I like to think that it is just what Kayla said! The Rays of God.

Chapter 22

Monday, November 11, 2002. Not much was new. I had 12 more treatments to go. It seemed like a lot even though it was much better than 36! But as sore and as tired as I was getting, 12 sounded like an awful lot. One of my bosses told me that day when I got to work that I looked tired. I felt tired.

I hadn't slept again the night before. Same old thing-worrying about everything. Christmas was coming, LP had to be paid, we had soooo many bills to pay. I couldn't shut my brain off. I got so tired of telling the kids that we didn't have money for them to do anything. It broke my heart. I wished I could take a day off here and there but I could not afford to. I wondered what would happen when I was really sore.

My husband works for a door manufacturer. They did a fundraiser for us. They put a slip in everyone's check asking for a voluntary donation. Although they did this in October, we hadn't seen any of the money yet. Tom thought

it was because no one gave. I had hoped that
wasn't the case. Not because we needed the
help, but because it would have made me sad
for the people he worked with to just not care.
He had other issues, too. To this day he hated
that they did this for us. He didn't want to accept
'charity' he called it. He was embarrassed. It
broke my heart. I tried to tell him, that one, we
needed the help and that wasn't our fault.
Certainly not his. Two, no one HAD to give us
anything. That is if they wanted to, they would.
And three, one day he will have the chance to
help someone else and will be able to-with no
questions asked! We eventually got a check for
over $600! Considering that most gave just 5 or 10
dollars, I thought that was very generous.
I was humbled once again by the generosity of
strangers.

Tuesday was a hectic day. I was running
behind most of the day. I even got to my
appointment late. Good thing about that,
I didn't have to wait to be called back. I then
found out I had to go to the simulation room for
the final planning of my treatment. This room is
where they figure out all the mathematical parts,
all the angles ,everything. I got one last tattoo.
After the radiation I was now getting, I would
have eight days of a 'boost' that would target
the tumor bed area. (When they told me that,
I thought what a stupid name for it. Bed. A bed is

an inviting thing, somewhere you go for comfort, not a place for some horrible tumor!) The area they would boost would probably get even more red. But after Friday the rest of the area that was done would be getting better. They gave me a more powerful burn cream in anticipation of my upcoming crispiness. They offered me pain pills. Yes, it was red, but pain pills? No thanks.

Remember the movie Groundhogs Day? You know the one, when the same day played over and over again. I thought that that was happening to me. Only it was a Monday over and over again. It was becoming one heck of a week. We had someone in to look at a basement water problem, our refrigerator went out, the district auditor was at work when I got there, so I got out of there late…it just went on and on.

It was just Wednesday and I had just 10 more to go. But I was so sore that this day I could actually feel it when they turned on the machine. Burn the burn some more. Yup, what a week I was having.

When I got home, we got one of those 'this is not a bill' from the insurance company for radiation treatments for the month of October. Holy Moly!! I could have bought a new car for what that cost. I was very grateful for insurance and I wondered how those people without it ever made it through this.

Someone told me that day that I had such a positive attitude. I got to thinking about that. I couldn't imagine being any other way. Sure I had my moments of sadness and anger-I still do. But what purpose would it serve me to go through life with anything but a positive attitude? None that I could see. Without it, you would just be grumpy and not enjoy the things and the people around you. So what would be the point of not being positive? I chose to look at life in the positive way, regardless of what I was going through or had already gone through. I chose to see the good. Considering the life I had had so far, I could be pretty darn grumpy. Instead I enjoy every day, immensely. I also learned to never complain about another birthday again. When my birthday rolls around, I am thankful for another year, another number. I would shout my age out to the world if I were asked. When you are faced with possibly not having another birthday, suddenly those numbers that most are afraid of, are music to your ears!

Chapter 23

Thursday, November 14, 2002. The armpit area was now blistered. And it hurt. A lot. I had only one more time for that area and then it was boost only. I couldn't imagine not having to go to the Cancer Center every single day.

I had an IEP meeting for Jamie that day. You know, I had done these meetings for 12 years. For 12 years I had to sit and listen, then tell them what I wanted for him, had to fight for inclusion and everything else. Most times I was a very strong person. You had to develop a backbone to be able to get through some of these meetings. This time I came to tears. I couldn't believe it. They started talking about what I wanted for his future and what job or living situation we wanted for him after high school and that we needed to start preparing him for it now. I just broke down and said what I wanted was to just be here for it. It must have been the stress of the week catching up to me. Or maybe the reality of it all. Jamie was another big reason I felt I needed to be around awhile. To fight his fight, to make sure he got the life he deserved and just wasn't put away somewhere. It was like one of his elementary teachers told all the middle school teachers during one particularly stressful planning meeting. She stopped their questions and complaining and simply said. "All children matter." Yes they do...All people matter. Period.

In my guest book on my site, many people wrote a lot and offered support and jokes and what not. One of them was a girl who worked with my sister and whose mom happened to be a patient at the cancer center, too. For some reason she always called my sister Jo-Bob so she called me Joy-Bob. This say I told her she would have to be changing mine to Bernie-Bob, translated BURN-ie Bob for those who didn't get that! I was getting so burned people were now commenting on it. They could see it because my neck was also now red. I would just show them the part that was really burned and shock them all. "Oh Joy' was pretty much the only comment I would get after they drew in their breath upon seeing the burns.

Friday came and so did my appointment. I was unexpectedly sent to my doctor because the techs did not like the look of my burns. They gave me more cream and pain pills this time to be taken as needed and I was told I was off work until further notice, until I had time to heal.

The doctor figured for at least a week. Great. What was I supposed to do for money now? The holidays were coming up, not to mention the normal stuff like bills and oh, food! I had to take my doctor's excuse to work and give it to the boss. He wasn't too happy about it. I got upset and started crying. I couldn't help it. Didn't he think I would rather be at work all day every day rather than go through what I was going through? He finally said you gotta do what you gotta do. Well no kidding! I would think my health came first.

On the way out I 'ran' into one of the girls there who was retiring that next Tuesday. She was one of the nicest, sweetest ladies I had ever met. I hugged her good-bye and cried harder. I then ran into another lady who worked there, whose husband was going through his second bout of fighting cancer, one he would lose. She told me her husband said he didn't know how I was working with all that pain anyhow and told me to go home and just get better.

Sunday I was up early after not sleeping very well again the night before. It was still hurting a lot, still blistering. In some spots the skin looked very dark, kind of like burned toast. It was starting to peel a lot under my arm.

Monday at my appointment I had to wait. Their computers went down so they were way behind. They gave us the option of rescheduling or waiting. Some people chose not to wait. But I wanted to get done on the day I was originally supposed to get done. There was no choice for me. Luckily I had nothing else to do. So I waited. And it ended up being only about an hour past my scheduled time. It went fast because I ended up chatting with some of the others who were also waiting. The people at the cancer center brought us doughnuts and cookies because they felt bad about making us wait. I didn't eat any as good as they looked, I just wasn't hungry. So only 7 more to go at this point. I was still so sore and imagined I would be for awhile. I was still blistering and peeling and turning colors, but was assured that was all normal. I was amazed at how much it hurt.

Tuesday. 6 more left! I had a couple people that day ask if I was counting them down. You bet! But then I had been all along. I had to wait for a long time to get called back this day and I got extremely tired. Of course then I was in there for my 30 second shot of radiation, then back to the waiting room. It was Tuesday-doctor day you know. He looked at my skin and said it was worse, which was to be expected. There was no sign of infection yet so that was good, but to watch it. He gave me a prescription for pain pills to take if I needed them. I only took them at night because they made me sleepy and I had too much to do during the day.

I went home and let myself have one of those moments again. I had been trying to clean the sore, blistering area and just getting a look at that along with the 'butch' hair I now had, well I couldn't take it at the moment. I cried. Again. Sometimes I still could not believe my new reality.

Chapter 24

Wednesday November 20, 2002. One more down. Five to go. I could count them on one hand! I was so looking forward to one week from them. One short week and treatments were finally done!

I was amazed at what skin could go through. I was still sore of course. I told my sister's co-worker she needed to change my name again, this time to Krispie-Bob. Because that was what I was at the moment. I was feeling pretty crispy.

I found myself at one point in the day saying, out loud, OWIE OWIE OWIE! It hurt that much!

Thursday, only 4 more left and then I decided it was all up to God. My armpit was looking better as it was done being radiated. It was still peeling and sore, but I would take the improvement.

Friday-33 down and 3 to go! It was the last time I had to tell them to have a nice weekend! It was getting so close I could taste it! The man who always went ahead of me each day was finished with his treatment this day. He had had 33 of them. He told me good luck, but he had to write it on a piece of paper, since he had no voice box. Two weeks earlier his wife had lost her battle with cancer. Yes, it could always be worse, couldn't it?

The blistering seemed to be done. At least on the armpit area. I didn't know yet if it would blister on the spot they were boosting. It was still peeling and red but as long as it was doing what it was supposed to, it was all good.

On my way home, I stopped into work to pick up my little Christmas bonus. I saw the boss. He gave me grief about it 'must be nice to sit at home and put your feet up and watch your soap operas.' I know he thought he was funny, but I failed to see the humor. I told him, "Look honey, I would trade you anytime! This has not been fun!" (I wasn't watching soap operas either, by the way. It was hard to get me in that chair for very long. Then I channel surfed anyhow. Must have a short attention span!)

Saturday I took a trip with a friend of mine to the Mall of America. I know some wondered how I could do that if I wasn't allowed to work. It was actually easy because my arm hurt more when I was sitting and it was rubbing. It felt good to go and pretend everything as normal. I was just shopping! No doctors or appointments or anything. Just shopping. Mind you I was shopping the clearance sections, but it was fun just the same.

Monday, November 25, 2002. Only two treatments to go. I could not believe it. One. Two. Before I was called back, I sat and chatted with a few people in the waiting room. One lady asked another one how she was. She said fine, then added, "If that is true, then why am I here?" I knew I would miss this part of coming here every day.

As I was laying for my 25-30 seconds of treatment, I got to thinking, only two more and the biggest grin came across my face. The techs probably thought I was crazy. Yes, they could see me. They kept a camera on you at all times so they could keep an eye on you, just in case you might need them.

One of the techs wondered what miracle cream I had put on my burns, because I kid you not there was that much of an improvement since Friday. The area where it wasn't being treated looked super. The boost area was still red, but also better.

They heard at work that I went shopping. Boy does news travel fast. I felt like I was back in high school. They couldn't figure out how I couldn't

work but I could go shopping. I had a burn that they didn't want to get infected and it hurt, that was why I wasn't working. The co-manager was sure I would just be too tired to shop. I always had told her I wasn't more tired or fatigued than usual. I had always fallen asleep in my chair- that came just from getting not enough sleep ever. I had thought it would be good to get some exercise and get out and being upright most of the day actually helped the burn out.
I got frustrated because people just didn't get it. I guessed my life away from there was just that and so was my health.

Tuesday. ONE more to go. I had my last Tuesday doctor's visit. I signed all my papers so that when I was done the next day all I would have to do is leave. I did have follow-up appointments on December 26th to see both oncology doctors and to talk about what was next and to check on how everything was healing. I was also scheduled still to have the expanders taken out and the implants put in on December 30th so I would have to have a pre-surgery physical on the 23rd. In the meantime, I had one whole month with NO appointments. None. I am not sure I would know how to act.

Wednesday, November 27, 2002. Final treatment day. Thank the Lord it was finally here. I couldn't help but think back on the year that I had had. I had come so far from May 31st when I heard those words I would never forget, "I have some tough news for you," to now, so many months later, coming to the end of my treatments. At one point I could not imagine ever getting to this point. Especially at the beginning, back when I couldn't imagine what chemo or radiation would be like, even though you hear about that kind of stuff all the time. I couldn't imagine all the doctor's appointments and how it felt to hear everything that I have had to endure hearing from them. I couldn't imagine the nightmare of losing my hair and being thrilled to shave my legs again.

But here I was. I was excited, terrified, happy, sad, and scared all at the same time. I would get to leave and pretend for awhile that things were like they always were. I knew I would always have that fear in the back of my mind , like all of us who have gone through this, the fear that it would return. I still carry that fear to this day. I always pray that it will never return. Always. I knew I will have those bad days and those moments again. And I knew I could work through them. I would forever be amazed at how people, even complete strangers helped out at times like this. I would forever be humbled by it. I would always be thankful for the prayers and support that I got and I prayed it would always be there. I knew now that I had to let the little things go.

That they are just not that important. I never wanted to forget that.

In my journal, I asked everyone at noon that day, to raise a glass, imaginary or otherwise, to say a toast, or like me, a prayer of gratitude. I was grateful to be done. I was grateful to have the doctors I was blessed to have and the medicine that was now available to them. I was mostly grateful to still be around, to be able to tell everyone thank you and to tell them I loved them.

Jo and Tom came with me that last time. I wanted to celebrate when I was done. I could hardly wait to leave. Yes I got my certificate of completion just like everyone else. You know what I think of that. When it was time to leave, I was happy, ecstatic, I ran out of there, dancing and singing. I was not sad like so many told me I would be. I knew I wasn't going to be actively fighting this anymore, at least not with medicine. But I did long ago what my cousin did, I looked to the heavens and said to God, "Thy Will Be Done!" I was going to be okay. Jo took us out to lunch to celebrate. A better lunch there never was.

The day remained a bit bittersweet for me, though, as I was finishing up with all of this, my cousin was only beginning her journey through this again. I told her to keep the faith and you do get done with the treatments. I know I was ready for something else to define my life.

The next day was Thanksgiving! What a glorious day. It took a whole new meaning on for me that year that has never gone away. The joy I felt I cannot describe to you. It was immense. Yes, I was Thankful. And I would remember to always say that prayer I said. Not one of please, I need or I want, But one of Thanks. For my family, my friends, my life.

Chapter 25

Sunday, December 1, 2002. I slept through the night for the first time in a very long time. I woke up thinking it would be the usual time in the middle of the night, but when I looked at the clock it said 5:17 a.m. It felt great. I was thankful to sleep all night because when I woke up sometimes I would think about it all. The reality. The future. All of it. About how I looked so different now but felt the same inside. I thought about my kids. I would hope that it was true that the further I got away from treatment, those kind of thoughts became fewer. Although I knew they would never completely go away. How could they? I thought, Gee, what a great thing to happen to a natural born worrier!

At least I was still able to laugh at things. At work someone asked this guy if he used to have long hair. He said yes, but he went from long hair to shaving it. So I said, "Yeah, Me too!" Then we all laughed. It's all you can do sometimes.

Tuesday, and back to not sleeping. I was trying to do my normal stuff like before but it was hard to keep my mind off the other stuff.
I longed for before all this happened to me when my worries were just the everyday worries like everyone has. I would look in the obituaries every day glad that the people I had met during all of this were not in there, hoping they were winning their battle, thinking that maybe more of us were winning the battle with this disease than losing to it. Hoping anyhow.

But then, I would read of those that have lost it. Including a girl from a small town close to here that I had been reading about. It made me very sad for her family. It just didn't seem right at all. I hated that children got this disease and that they had to suffer. I hated that they died from it.

I was driving home from the store and saw the 'Rays of God' again. It made me smile to see those and it always made me feel good inside. I will be forever grateful to Kayla for thinking of that as a child and sharing it with me.

I was trying to take it one day at a time, like always. I was still praying that I would see all my kids graduate, get married, see my grandchildren and be there for them whenever they would need me. It scared me still that that might not happen.

I wanted people to know I was still happy. Even with all those thoughts. They just couldn't help but pop into my head. I am pretty sure that is normal. Christmas was coming, and I loved that time of year, and although money was tight, I didn't worry about having a nice Christmas at all. We were going to be together, and that is all that mattered.

Friday, December 6, 2002. This was looking to be the very first week since my whole ordeal started way back in May, that I was actually going to be able to work my normal schedule every single day. No appointments, no being sick, no taking time off. Just working. I was getting my office back in order to where everything was before and where everything should be. The manager one day came on the intercom before we opened and said, "Do you notice these days how Joy starts everything with, If it is where it's supposed to be... I got on the intercom and told him politely to Shut up! I got to thinking, there probably wasn't too many places you could do that and still have a job.

Saturday. Just finished my first full week of work since it had all started. That felt good. My office was looking great. My burn was almost all gone, including the boost area. I was hoping it would be all healed for my surgery that was scheduled in three weeks. I didn't like the thought of being put under again, at all. It made me rather nervous. I also had a follow up appointment at the cancer center coming up and I was already dreading that. I just had to trust that I would be fine. I felt fine, but then I felt fine before, too, when there was cancer in my body.

Friday December 13, 2002. I had an appointment at the plastic surgeon's office to discuss my upcoming surgery. We talked about the surgery, decided on the size of the implants. Let me tell you, if that isn't a strange thing to do, to be able to pick out what size you want to be! I had to return in one week to go over consent and then the 23rd, I had a pre-surgery physical. Then you know, back to the appointment on the 26th to hear again, "Because of the size of your tumor and your age, blah blah" By then I KNEW what size it was and all the other crap that they had to say along with it. I also realized that day it was 6 months since they had taken that 'large' tumor out of me. A half a year already. Amazing.

The next day Kayla and I went to a movie. Could I just sit there and enjoy it? Of course not. I wish I could turn off my mind sometimes. Why couldn't I just sit and enjoy the movie with my daughter instead of thinking about everything I had been through and everything that was to come? Why did I have to worry about the future so much? I wanted so badly to be able to just turn my mind off. I was trying but I will tell you, the mental part of this journey I was on was sometimes the toughest part of all.

Chapter 26

Monday, December 16, 2002. Kayla and I finished Christmas shopping. I was so worried that I would even be able to do that. But thanks to the wonderful generosity of someone, I was. There is this person every year, who picks one family who she feels needs some help and puts money in a card. That year she picked us. It was so humbling to once again be at the receiving end of such generosity. I always said thank you, but it just never seemed like enough. I wanted to convey to people how much everything they did for not only me, but my family, meant!

Two weeks until surgery and the anticipation of it all was getting bad. Sometimes I think it was harder than the actual surgery. I just couldn't imagine being almost normal again!

Tuesday. The weather was rotten, but what can you expect in Iowa in December? I tried to be thankful anyhow, you know for another day. I appreciated every one. But I could still hate snow!

The thoughts were still popping into my head. I knew it would take time and I hoped that time was something I had a lot of. I was still new to all this, so I didn't think I could really be expected to forget.

Wednesday, December 18, 2002.It was the news again. All the time, in my face. Was it like that before? I couldn't remember, but it seemed like it was about breast cancer all the time now. The latest was a winner. They had a story on about how Christmas was hard for women who had had breast cancer. WHAT? (Didn't you hear me yelling at the tv?) I couldn't believe it. Christmas and life for that matter is what you make of it. I loved it and was having a fabulous time. (Think of Jim Carrey in the Grinch yelling "FABULOUS! That would be me!) We just had such a great time around my house each and every day. My kids constantly were telling me that I was crazy. I always told them and still do that it makes life more interesting. I just got so tired of hearing about breast cancer all the time. It was hard enough to get it out of my mind, I didn't need the constant reminders.

Thursday it was to the plastic surgeon again. I was put into a five year study. It was the only way to get the kind of implants that they were going to use. These were new ones from a different company and they were very excited. Only 50 doctors in the whole country and 1000 women would be accepted. One of those women was me.

Monday I had my physical. Blood pressure- great. The doctor told me she had gotten progress reports as I went through all my treatments and everything and that they ALL sounded good. That was nice to hear. So one more week until surgery. I couldn't wait until it was over.

Thursday December 26, 2002. Our Christmas had been wonderful. I already had all of our decorations put away with the exceptions of my angels. They still sit out to this day.

I went to my appointments at the cancer center. My doctor was so nice and he always made me feel so much better. I appreciated that. He talked about the kind of cancer I had. HAD. Did you hear that? HAD!!! PAST tense! I didn't know one little tiny three letter word could make me feel so wonderful! Had had had had had! Okay, I know that's enough! (Had!)

Since one of my hormone receptors was (slightly)positive I would be on Tamoxifen for the next five years. This is a hormone blocker. Supposed to help reduce the chances of reoccurrence. I would do whatever it took to do that. It pretty much meant that at age 44 I would be put into early menopause. Great. I needed to buy a new shirt. "I am still hot, only now it just comes in flashes!"

I would have checkups every four months for the first two years, then every six months for a couple of years. I loved it when he talked about all the years ahead of me. I could have cried. He explained the checkups. They basically just did blood tests unless the liver enzyme check was the least bit out of whack. And that didn't even mean something necessarily, as a cold or alcohol could change that. If that test showed anything then they would do a CT scan, but they didn't do those routinely. Good, I thought.

From there it was over to the radiology checkup. Same thing. They were not going to do anything else, come back in 4 months! My skin looked wonderful. I even graduated so to speak to a physician's assistant there instead of the regular doctors.

One of the doctors asked me if it wasn't nice to have it all behind me now? Oh you just don't know! The other one told me that I was now on cruise control. I was so thankful to be at this point. I knew the checkups would be scary, but in between, I could get somewhat back to normal. Or what was passing as normal to me those days.

Monday, December 30, 2002. Had to be at the hospital at 6a.m. for surgery. The nurse who wheeled me into the operating room was playing with my hair!! Yup, you heard that right! She said it looked curly in back and said it was really thick. (I even walked out of that hospital with no bandana and no wig!)

It turned out to be a rough day. When I woke up in recovering I was shocked to see that I was sleeping on my side. The nurse said that they couldn't keep me on my back. I also decided when I woke up that throwing up would be a lot of fun. Ouch. They handed me a basin and sent me home. I was sore, uncomfortable and had to have a binder on the keep things in place for a week. That was tight and uncomfortable.
I slept in my recliner again. Could not lay down in bed. That made my lower legs ache a lot.
I tried eating but was light headed and even had a major headache. I began wondering if having boobs again was really worth all of this! Oh! This is the message my husband , dear man, put on my website for all to read.

Monday, December 30, 2002. at 4:01 p.m.

Hello,

The bunnies are in the hutch. She was out of surgery a little after 9 and back to her room at 11. Home at 2.

Tom

I am sure he thought he was cute!

Someone told me at the hospital that my hair looked like I had a Mia Farrow thing going on. Real short bangs, etc. Daniel must not have liked it at home that I was running around FINALLY without anything on my head, because he told me to put my bandanna back on. I told him NOPE. I was finally free of all that stuff. I didn't like how short the hair was but it was hair!

As for the bunnies in the hutch comment from dear hubby. It came from my cousin calling them blouse bunnies. So he decided they were now in the hutch. Such a funny man. He thinks!

The next day was my wedding anniversary. I got to spend it recuperating in my chair. I did tease Tom that I least I got him a present!

Wednesday I tried to sleep in the bed again, No such luck. Back to the recliner. My legs hurt all night long. I would get up and walk around, trying to make them feel better. I would try sitting down and laying down, but they would just hurt more. The pain meds I had were too strong for that. They had made me dizzy the last time I took them, so it was back to Tylenol. I know I tossed and turned in that chair, it was hard to get comfortable. I am such a side sleeper that trying to sleep in a chair was impossible.

I wasn't allowed to lift anything so I would get frustrated looking around at things that needed done. Here I was again, back to being dependent on others for awhile. I didn't like it any better than the first time around. Little did I know, it wouldn't be the last time either. This was all far from over.

Chapter 27

Friday, January 3, 2003. My last day of quiet before I had to return to work. I was going to try to enjoy it. I wasn't really ready to go back to work yet, but I had to. I slept in the chair part of the night, thinking the bed wouldn't work. Tom had to get up at 3 so I went into my bed and I slept comfortably. I even remember dreaming. I dreamed of my aunt Jean. She had died in 1986 at age 52 of cancer. I missed her a lot. I remember dreaming of her for a long time that night. It was just like we were having a wonderful visit. I like to think that just maybe we were.

I got a letter from my doctor the day before with my blood work results for surgery. She thought that I would like to know that they were normal. She was right, I had been wondering about them. It was hard to open that paper and read it. She did write a very nice note. I really like my doctor!

I was feeling a bit better by now, still a little light-headed. I started the Tamoxifen that day so

I would know within a couple weeks if I got any severe hot flashes. I hoped I didn't have to deal with those.

Sunday. I was thinking a lot about what I had went through and what all had changed for me. What it meant. Those great words of the doctor, you know the ones, 'the cancer you HAD' were ringing in my ears. I would much rather have those words ringing in my ears than the ones I had heard so long ago. The actuality of it all got to me. At my age, I was talking about the cancer I had. It was something we never expect so young. And I had actually had it. Putting my mind around that sometimes was very hard. I knew I had been through the worst. But it was funny, how I had also been through the best times and had some wonderful things happen to me. It was strange how you could go through the worst thing physically and try to be your healthiest, you feel the crappiest as they try to heal you. It is the scariest of times, but you have to remain optimistic.

Monday came and I didn't go back to work. I thought it would be hard to put things back into order as I couldn't lift anything or bend. The compression bandage was giving me so much grief. I never had anything so uncomfortable on ever. It kept putting the 'right one' to sleep. I had to call work and the boss didn't have much to say. Sometimes he was so good during all this and sometimes he just didn't get it. I don't think he really had a clue how hard all of this really was. It wasn't just him either, I don't think a lot of people really understood.

I returned to work on Tuesday. My office was just as I expected. A total mess and I couldn't fix it by myself. I had to have someone come in and do all the lifting for me. My co-manager walked in, took one look around, and said, 'welcome back.'

But my big accomplishment at this time? My shining moment? I went to the American Cancer Society and donated my wigs, scarves, and anything else for my head I didn't need. I could not believe I actually got brave enough to walk out into the world without my head covered at all. I figured it was time. But I was shocked at how hard it was. I was very self-conscious. I am sure that people weren't staring. Why would they? How could they know I had anything other than short hair??? Of course there was some I knew that I got looks from, like the lady I saw each week at the post office window. Everyone at work was great. They commented on how thick and wavy it was. And that it was a different color. Told me how much they liked it. Considering it was now January in Iowa, my head was now very cold. I did have to have a hat for outdoors to keep warm.

I couldn't believe how the hair was now constantly a topic of discussion. Many times. Every day. I got nothing but compliments and comments about how wavy and dark it was. I didn't know how long I would grow it out before I had to color it again. I was not used to having it this color at all. No it wasn't only black now, but black and white. Before I lost my hair? Straight, not a curl in it and reddish brown. And seeing that I will always be a redhead at heart I was looking forward to the day I was again. I was enjoying the freedom of no wigs or scarves or anything. It did take a long while to get used to going out without that protection. You felt like everyone was staring at you. I was considering soaking my head in Miracle Gro!

The compression bandage was now gone. I got to change it to a sports bra that still did the job.

Tuesday, January 14, 2003. Back to the doctor to get my stitches out. Nifty how they just snip each end and pull. Everything looked great and doctor said 'they' were where 'they' needed to be. That was a relief. I had to return in a month for a checkup.

So I was free for a whole month. No appointments, no checkups! Nothing of any kind for a month. Woohoo!

Of course they commented on my hair,
who didn't? My mom even got to see it as she
stopped by that day. She liked it short, of course.

Jamie was sitting at his computer right after
his bath, hair clean. He looks at me, touches his
head and says, "How's my hair look mom?" I
almost rolled on the floor laughing. For him to say
this, is amazing. Especially a question. I loved it.
I wondered if he wasn't actually talking about
my hair instead of his, that maybe it was his way
of acknowledging it. Or maybe, he just thought
he looked good!

Wednesday, the boss wanted me to stay and
help with inventory. Remember how I said he just
didn't get it? Case in point! My arm was aching
by 10 that morning. I was wondering if I would
ever be able to do the things again that I had
done before. I thought probably not all. I didn't
like it. This was all frustrating enough, but when
others saw me and figured I was the same as
before because I was done with treatments and
all, it became even more frustrating.

My big toes even hurt that day. Okay, not
to gross you out but you are about to learn one
more thing that chemo can do to you. It can
kill off your nails. I was lucky. It just attacked my
big toenails. They were definitely dead, but not
coming off. It was ugly. And it hurt. Was that

more than you ever wanted to know? Me too. It just amazed me all of the things that chemo does to a body. The things it could change. The things it did change.

Friday. I was looking in the mirror. I could hardly believe what I saw. It was me. But it didn't feel like it. I couldn't help but stare. The me I knew , the one I felt I was, had disappeared several months before. It struck me how you could change so much on the outside and feel the same on the inside. But then, I thought, do I really feel the same on the inside? I highly doubted it. Nothing was quite the same. Nothing. But then I guess I didn't expect it to be.

Chapter 28

Sunday, January 19, 2003. I kept forgetting. That my hair was short that is. Until I saw my reflection somewhere. It always surprised me. I was thinking about 'stuff' again and thinking back to an article an AP reporter had written so long ago , mentioning my long mane of red hair. Wow, that seemed like a lifetime ago. (Of course most days, many things seemed like a lifetime ago!) I often wondered if I would ever have that long mane of hair again.

Tuesday. I had one of 'those moments' again that morning. I thought maybe I should just do away with mirrors. You could almost feel like your old self , well, kind of, but then you look in a mirror and POW! Who the heck was that thing looking back? It was such a strange thing. I wondered what in the world had happened to me.

Friday, January 24, 2003. I wondered in my journal online if people had moved on or were still checking on me. I wondered what they wanted to hear about. Did they want me to say

I was fine? I hoped I was fine. I felt I was. And I hoped I would stay that way for a long long time. But I would wonder, what would I do if it someday came back, this cancer. It was only natural to think about that. You get reminded of it so much. Not just of what I went through-though sometimes that already felt like a bad dream. Well it was a nightmare, truly.

My hair wasn't growing back fast enough for me. I hated seeing it so short. Yes, I was glad it was growing, of course, but it seemed so slow. I wanted to look more like what I did before all this happened. Not like I just had cancer. I didn't want people looking at me funny.

I was getting so tired of people saying, "How are you feeling today?" Don't get me wrong, I appreciated all of everyone's concern. But you would get those that would look at you with such pity and ask in their own special tone. "How are YOU feeeelllling today?" I wanted to scream some days. I AM FINE. DON'T YOU GET IT? I HAD cancer! HAD. Remember? HAD. I had it treated, got rid of it. I was fine. Just like you and you and you and........Sure the arm ached every single day and I couldn't do everything that I used to and that made me mad but in the way that counted I was fine!

I had been on the Tamoxefin for 3 weeks. My weight was still the same and I had no major hot flashes. I would just wake up very warm once in awhile. If that was the most I had to deal with that was great because I knew some people had some very bad side effects on this. I only had 4 years, 11 months and 1 week to keep taking it!

Monday, February 3, 2003. I see in the paper yet another person I had met during radiation had died. That made 4 so far. Which to me was a lot considering that I was only there for 7 weeks and only for a few minutes each day on most days. It made me incredibly sad. She was one funny, feisty lady. It also made me mad. I wanted this disease to go away. It took too many people. And I hated it. Every time you read about someone in the paper dying from cancer you couldn't help but feel a bit more nervous. That has been a feeling I get to this day. It's hard to know why some survive and some don't.

Sunday, February 9, 2003. A beautiful sunrise. I always enjoyed them but so much more now. It may sound cliché but it is so true. Lost my big toenail. Gross. A new one was growing underneath already. Gosh, the effects of chemo, even many months later!

I found out when I got my insurance papers about my last surgery that a payment was made to Pathology Associates. WHAT?! Of course I called my surgeon. Seems it was routine to send the expander and capsule from around where the tumor was to be checked. It had to be okay or I would have heard long before that. Great and fine and all, but a little warning before I saw that would have been nice. I don't like to be kept in the dark about anything and this was still very nerve wracking at times.

Monday, February 10, 2003. I went to the Relay for Life kickoff breakfast. I decided this year I was participating. I needed to give back, to help others, to do whatever I could. I always would. I signed up Team Joy. (for lack of a better team name!) I put out the call for team members and got to work. I learned there would be music, food, fun and entertainment. But the thing I was looking forward to the most? The cancer survivor victory lap. The Relay was described as a 'place where friends, family and loved ones join to celebrate survivorship and to honor those who have lost the battle." Pass me the Kleenex! I knew I was going to need some.

Chapter 29

Tuesday, February 11, 2003. The planning for the Relay , to be held in June, was coming along great. Kayla was the first to sign up and donate. She gave the rest of her birthday money. I was so proud of her. I put out a call for names because on our site we were going to have a poster of who we were walking for. The first part would say…WE WALK IN HONOR OF: we had four names so far, me, my cousin Judy, my aunt Alice and my uncle Ed. Below that would be IN MEMORY OF. With too many names, in my opinion. I had already collected, Tom's dad, Jim, my aunt Jean, my uncle Jim, my aunt Mary Lou, my grandma Lois, Tom's aunt Opal, Tom's uncle Jack and a friend, Lyle. Did I tell you how much I hate this disease? I know I did, but I can't help but repeat it. It has taken too many people from us.

Friday February 14, 2003. Valentine's day. And I spend it at the hospital. Did you think just because I got my permanent implants in I was done? Ha! Nope, we had 'finishing touches' to go. When I told my boss I needed the day off he kept asking why. So I told him. Quote. "I am going to go have the pointers put on." He turned so red. I laughed so hard. You see, think about it, they took everything I had. Which includes the nipples. And if I wanted to look half-way normal the plastic surgeon had to make me some new ones. More than you ever wanted to know I am sure. There was also a bit of skin where it was sewn together on my left side, that needed to be trimmed down, so he would do that at the same time.

I arrived at the hospital at 6 a.m. I walked down to the operating room around 7:20. I chose not to be sedated. I was tired of waking up and throwing up. So I would just be numbed and given a local and be awake the whole time. The nurse who was walking me down to the operating room, chose to share with me that a lady had chose the same option just the day before. Then she shared that this lady 'freaked out'. I don't know about you, but that isn't exactly the thing I needed to hear walking into the operating room!

The doctor came in and gave me the local. Or so he tried. He kept testing the area to be operated on, on the side. I kept feeling it. He did this about 3 or 4 times. He did construct the nipples while talking about his daughter and her boyfriend. I could feel blood dripping that is about all. But then he gets to the side where he needs to cauterize the skin. (Ah the smell of burning flesh once again.) Anyhow, I felt it once, twice, then OUCH! Wow, did that hurt. He said something about a blood vessel and having to go further than he thought he would. The nurse told me to cuss at him. Cuss at him? He was lucky I couldn't jump off the table and hurt him.

He was finally done, I sat up walked by the surgery waiting room, back to my little room, asked for coffee and 20 minutes later I was on my way home. Out by 9a.m. Tom took me to breakfast. I had to thank him, it was nice, but there I was sitting with no makeup and operating room head. The epitome of glamour, let me tell you! We stopped for pain pills and antibiotics and home I went.

I got home and Chris had made them cinnamon muffins for breakfast, from scratch, made us a pie for Valentine's day and had done the laundry and the dishwasher. What a kid.

I often joked that year that for our anniversary I got new boobs and for Valentine's day, I got new nipples. Yippee. Can you imagine presents like that?

Monday, February 17, 2003. I was still very sore. I took the bandages off the day before. I was surprised at how much I had bled. There was one spot I thought looked like it was still bleeding a bit. I knew I would be glad when I was healed from this round of surgery. I almost could feel sorry for myself. But then I read the paper.

Proof that you never know what's going to happen and that life is much too short. Saturday a 43 year old was killed in a snowmobile accident. An older man was found dead in his yard from exposure. And that Sunday, a 26 year old mother of two young girls ages 3 and 6 MONTHS was killed when she hit a guard rail near the Mason City exit by our house. My sister's and nieces and us had literally just passed that spot before it happened. "By the Grace of God....." Be thankful for every single day. Tell those you love that you do. Don't stress over things you can do nothing about. Live your life to the fullest. It IS just too damn short.

Chapter 30

Wednesday, February 19, 2003. I was healing a bit more each day. I would be glad to be all healed. Again. This had been surgery number 5 since June and I thought that was quite enough for awhile. It is amazing what a body can go through. Mine went through all those surgeries, the chemo, and the radiation and it healed each time. What a blessing that was I thought.

I ran into an old classmate at work. I literally bumped into her on purpose. She looked right at me and said, Oh I am sorry, excuse me! I said Hello! And she finally saw who I was. She said You cut your hair! Nope, I obviously hadn't this time. So now I was in disguise-people who had known me for years were not recognizing me.

I got a call from the Relay for Life chairman. They had put out a call for nominations for Honorary Chair of the Relay. He said that they got many for me and asked me to be the Honorary Chair. Of course I said yes.

I made an unexpected visit to my doctors office on Thursday. Seems like I had a little fluid around my stitches. Nothing to worry about so they told me. I couldn't wait until I got those out. They were bothering me.

Monday February 24, 2003. I had a bit of a grumpy day. Guess I was due one. Thinking about lots of things. Everything. Even thinking about the first call I got from the doctor to tell me I had this and how that felt. I thought about the disbelief and everything that had happened to me since then. It was sometimes easy to go through the everyday things and try to think that it was all a bad dream. How, in fact, could this have happened to me anyhow? It certainly wasn't a part of ANY of my plans! It was hard to wonder and to worry. I would look at my kids and sometimes just want to cry. I wanted a guarantee that I would be there for them for a long long time. I know none of us has that guarantee and yes, we could walk out and get hit by that bus, fine, but my odds were now just a little different. So I was having one of those days. Didn't need anyone to tell me to cheer up. I wasn't depressed or unhappy or anything. I was just thinking about stuff.

Wednesday, February 26, 2003. HAPPY BIRTHDAY TO ME!!! What a day! I decided I would always celebrate birthdays-always. I wouldn't hide my age. I would be glad for every single year! It was a great day. My sweet Kayla, who was only 11 at the time, made me a card. The front had pretty flowers and said 'happy birthday mom' all over the edges. Inside....

"Mom, I hope you have a very special birthday, and please do me a favor and live your life like you will never pass away and always live your life to the fullest...."

Wow, anyone got a Kleenex left to share???

March 2, 2003. Only got to get the stitches out of the left side when I went to the doctor. And OUCH thank you very much! They had to leave them in the radiated side for an extra week because it takes that tissue longer to heal. If they took them out early there would be the chance that it would split. Ick.

The other stitches came out on Thursday. I was glad as it was a bit sore. Daniel had been sick so he had to go to the doctor for a recheck. While we were there the doctor asked if we wanted a blood test to see if his counts were on the way up. Daniel said YES! (He is 13 at this time.) Not three minutes after the test, the doctor was in with the results. All counts had at least doubled and were well into the normal range. So Daniel grinned. I let out a sigh of relief. The doctor says, Now you don't need a bone marrow biopsy. YIKES! I was worried because I know all too much about blood counts. We got into the car and Daniel asked if I had understood what the doctor said. I said yes. All Daniel heard was 'bone marrow biopsy' I said Daniel, you DON'T need to have one. He was visibly relieved. Because unfortunately my kids also knew too much about blood counts.

Wednesday, March 12, 2003. Another busy week. Just normal busy. I liked that. I had been running into people who were seeing my hair for the first time. I got lots of compliments on it. I always got asked if it was that way before. Black and white and curly. No. Everyone seemed to want to touch it.

While I was out one day I was looking at birthday cards. One had a button in it that said it all for me. "I have survived damn near everything!" Surviving was good!

Friday, March 14, 2003. It was a beautiful day. The wind was blowing through my hair. Woohoo. MY hair, it was a great feeling. I could walk outside in the wind and not have to hold my 'hair' on. I loved it. The back was getting longer and curlier. People continued to touch it daily. My boss told me I looked like Pat Benatar. Rock and roll!

Tuesday. It was getting closer to that very first checkup. I tried not to think about it, but April was getting closer all the time. It was easy to put things out of your mind. Sometimes. But reality was always there. April would also be one full year since this ordeal had started. One year from the time I had the shooting pains, found the lump and well, you know the rest. Time truly goes by fast. I was glad for that. And I was glad that a year later, I was still around!

Chapter 31

Monday, March 24, 2003. Spring break underway, life cruising along again. Over the weekend I went to see one of my sisters. I bought hair color because every time I looked in the mirror and saw that black and white hair, I saw my mother looking back at me! Besides, I never had black hair in my life and it just didn't look like me. So I became a red head again! I loved it. I got lots of compliments on it. Even many were telling me how 'long' it was getting. I thought how funny your perspective changes on what is long and short.

I had tried to rake the yard. I used to actually enjoy doing that. Now it just pulled and started to feel uncomfortable. Do you know how much I really hated that? So then I had Tom fill the tire in Chris' bike and I raced around on that. That felt good.

Thursday was my long day at work. I always spent the whole day punching in orders on the computer. My arm always ached extra after that. It ached most all of the time anyhow. If you could draw a line down the middle of my body, it would divide the left side that always felt fine, and still does and the right side which always hurt or ached somewhere. And still does. I knew someday that I would get old and hurt and not be able to do stuff that I used to do. But not at 45. I was determined to not let it stop me. I had to learn to live with the aches and pains and to compensate in any way I could.

That night I had one of those moments again where I just couldn't believe all that had happened to me. I was glad that some things we could forget or at the very least let them go out of our mind some. I knew April was approaching fast with that first check up. I wanted it over with and wanted them to tell me everything was fine. I wanted to have four months ahead before worrying about it again.

Tuesday, April 1, 2003. Tom's 40th birthday. A busy month coming up. Relay meetings, dentist appointments, orthodontist appointments, checkup, appointment with the plastic surgeon. Something all the time.

Friday. Getting closer to that first check up. I found that it popped into my mind constantly at this point. Every ache and pain was a cause for pause and worry. I was told that that happened. I ran into a speech teacher from way back when

Jamie went to the hospital for speech. She told me her aunt had told her that the worst part of it all was the worry. Boy, did I know what she meant. I didn't know if that would ever go away. I didn't see how it could with checkups every 4 months. Plus I was hearing of so many others who would get breast cancer again. Even those who had negative nodes like me. I was hearing of others who hadn't won this battle. It was hard. I tried to remain positive and live my life like I had before. It just ached more to do it now. Just the day before every single joint ached, my arms ached, my foot tingled. I felt so much older. I just had to learn to live with it. Didn't mean I had to like it!

Thursday, April 10, 2003. You are about to learn even more about reconstruction I bet you didn't think about. Tattooing. Yup, you heard me. I had my appointment at the plastic surgeons for tattooing. Think about it. You learned he had to make nipples, right? Did you think about the color?! Ah.....I can hear you all now. Well, we picked out a color and proceed. Didn't you all hear me yelling OUCH? Okay, so I was only in my mind. For you see, my surgeon did not numb the area at all. He worked fast and furious to get them done. Oh Lord did that hurt! In my mind I am thinking, am I crazy????? I could have lived without this right? Wasn't looking as normal as possible highly overrated? Well, I lived through it. And I went home, sore, and bleeding. They covered them of course so they would heal. (There I was home healing from yet another procedure!) The surgeon told me once they would probably fade...and they have, that I could get them redone again. No thanks! I will live with how they look now.

I did get the okay to pretty much do what I wanted. I no longer had a weight limit restriction on what I could pick up. That was a great feeling. It didn't mean of course, it wouldn't bother me, it just meant I was healed enough and far enough from surgery that those babies were pretty much staying in place!

I had to laugh because when I shared about this appointment on my online journal I think I shocked quite a few people. Most people did not know about this part of it all. And why would you. If you didn't have this happen to you or to someone you knew, why would you have any reason for knowing or even thinking about it. I just never knew that my boobs, if you will, would be talked about so much on the internet! I did tell my doctor once that after having kids and then being through all this, pretty much all my privacy and dignity just went right out the window.

Chapter 32

Monday April 14, 2003. Busy time. And I liked that. I was joining the Relay Committee meetings since I was picked to be the honorary chair. I had no clue what I was supposed to do, but figured going to the meetings was a great way to find out. I was going to be interviewed by the newspaper as the honorary chair. They were going to tell my story. I also had to write a story of my own for the team captains to be put into a newsletter for them.

The newspaper reporter came on Tuesday and stayed for two hours. She not only talked to me but to Tom too and asked the kids to talk if they felt like it. They took a picture of me on my computer posting in my online journal. So not only would everyone get to read my story, but they would get to see me with my new short curly hair too! I just had to wait for the story to turn up in the paper and see how many stupid things I actually said!

Sunday, April 20, 2003. Easter. A day of faith. Something I felt I knew just a little about. My tattoos were about healed. I was glad that phase was all done. I had ten days to go until my checkup. I thought about that more each day as it got closer. Sometimes I was just in disbelief about it all. I still didn't know how in the world this had all happened to me.

My story finally ran on April 23. The headline read. "Cherishing every sunrise."

It came from the opening of the article. "When Joy Brown sees the sunrise from the farm fields surrounding her house on the outskirts of Mason City, she looks skyward and says a prayer.

'I see the sun coming up and I say "Thank you for another day,'" she said.

Last year at this time , Brown felt there might not be too many sunrises in her future. "

It then went on and told about me being diagnosed and everything I had to endure. It mentioned my age and my four young children. Talked about the call from the doctor.

Then, "Tom said, "We just looked at each other and teared up. I kinda knew what was up (during the call from the doctor) when I looked at her and tears were coming down."

For him, part of the shock was the realization that once again someone he loved had cancer. His father had died of brain cancer when Tom was 13."

More on treatments, support from people, using the internet, and my advice to woman.

Then, "She credits an uncle in Colorado, who she calls "'Miracle Ed', my second dad," for her formula for dealing with cancer-prayers, a positive attitude and humor. He was given two months to live after a liver cancer diagnosis but the disease disappeared.

"I never give up." Joy said...."We have such a good time here. I make sure the kids know I love them."

I got so much positive feedback on this article. People would mail it to me. I asked them at work to save it for me. When I went in it was gone and I asked about it. The co manager told me to look above the time clock. Our manager had the story matted and framed and hung in our break room. I thought that was pretty special.

Wednesday April 30th. Check up day. It felt strange to go in there again. And it was hard to. Although it was good to see some of the people who had helped me through this tough journey, it was hard to return to the Cancer Center. I got a lot of comments about the hair and the story.

I didn't even get to find out my test results that day and I didn't like it. Seems they scheduled me with the doctor on a day he wasn't even there! I was not too happy. It was hard enough to wait for these checkups I did not want to have to go home and stress again about coming back. I did get to go to my radiation check up. She thought my thyroid felt 'fleshy' so she had that checked out. It's always something isn't it. The good thing was she ordered blood tests so as long as those turned out okay I wouldn't return until my next regular check up. So they took my blood and I got to go home. And? Wait yet again. (Wait was rapidly becoming a four-letter word in my vocabulary!)

Friday, May 2. Around noon I got a call at work. It was the nurse in the doctor's office. She apologized for hunting me down. Said ALL the blood tests were NORMAL!! I think I did the happy dance about then. Not even a thyroid problem. She made me so nervous when she called. I could rest easy again for a few months. I had gotten my four month reprieve. I went into the break room and surprised myself when I told a co-worker that it all came back fine-I cried. Tears of joy. So much better than the other ones.

Chapter 33

I got to thinking again after this first checkup. I had thought I would have more support before I went to it. Or at the very least some well-wishes. Was that silly of me to notice or want that? Maybe need it. I didn't know. I just knew that everyone was there at the beginning of all this for me. This just felt so different. I had always known I was in this all alone. Now it really felt like I was.

But sometimes, why wouldn't I still want someone to hold my hand? Someone to say good luck, to say I love you, or I'm sorry. I thought it would be nice. Because sometimes it was still very hard. I never dreamed I would have to live like this. Not so soon anyhow. I didn't want to have to go to the cancer center, I didn't want to give them my blood. I didn't want to HAVE to do any of it. I had no choice. From this time for the rest of my life, I would always be going to some doctor giving them my blood and hoping and praying it was always good news.

You know I kept an online journal but I also kept one for me, one where I could tell how I really felt about some things. One where I wrote stuff that others might not want to hear. I guess I shielded a lot of people from many feelings I had.

At this point I thought all the reconstruction was done. To say I was underwhelmed by what I now had was probably an understatement. They certainly didn't look like the real things, no matter how hard the doctor tried to make them as close to normal as he could. Sure with a shirt on, I still looked like a girl and I was grateful for that. But without? I still saw the scars and I still noticed how different they looked. And they didn't feel the same either. Especially on the radiated side. It tended to feel a bit hard. The doctor said it might improve with time.

At the online support group we talked about this subject. One lady talked about how before they were such a part of her sex life. And now? They were gone. Which meant an important part of her sex life was gone too. I could relate. Imagine if you will, the feelings that they could produce being gone. Forever. Imagine your husband being a breast man and they are gone. Forever. Mine used to joke with me that if I ever got them reduced, he would divorce me. He liked them big. No other way to put it. And now? That part was gone. At least in the past I knew he wanted me. Now he was falling asleep every weekend on the couch or in the chair. Sometimes it felt to me like he was pulling away when I tried to kiss him, always making excuses. We had only been together twice in the year since it had started. TWO times. Period. I felt totally unwanted. It seemed like not only did this cancer rob me of part of my body, but part of my relationship with my husband as well. It made me angry. It hurt more than I can convey.

As time has gone on, of course it has improved. A bit. It took a very long time. I can report to you my husband is more attentive, but it is still different. It is not the same. We have talked about it many times. I will tell him how it feels to no longer have him touching me 'there'. I feel less of a woman, less desirable, that I have less to offer him. He even told me that it WAS different. That they didn't feel the same. It continues to be an issue we work on and work through.

Chapter 34

I am sure you all remember me talking about "Miracle Ed'. He is my uncle who was diagnosed with cancer, given a couple months to two years tops to live and he found out on the day I was diagnosed he was cancer free. He had gone in that day to see what they next step was and well, there was no cancer.

Let me tell you about this wonderful man. He married my aunt Mary. They met very young and were definitely soul mates and best friends for life. He was the best husband, father, uncle, friend, that I had ever met. I never knew anyone who was kinder. A loving gentle soul. Every time he talked to his girls on the phone, even if he just saw them, he always always told them he loved them.

When I heard about his diagnosis I was devastated. I had already lost too many family members to cancer. I did not want it to take another one. Little did I know our family would have two more of us diagnosed before the year was out!

Ed dealt with his diagnosis and treatment with faith first of all. Many people were praying for him. He dealt with it with love of course, from all of us. And he dealt with it with humor. Always joking with his nurses.

When I was diagnosed I knew I could look to Ed and to Mary for strength and for an example of just how I wanted to deal with my journey. I many times would get phone calls or cards in the mail, just to give me encouragement, to tell me I could do it. It meant the world to me.

Ed and Mary decided to take a cruise for their anniversary in May of 2003. Ed had not been feeling up to par before they left. So he took a blood test and they went on their vacation. When he got back he got the news, that the cancer had returned. It was devastating, I was angry. He had beaten this so why was it back? Why Ed? It wasn't fair. And it scared the hell out of me. If our prayers were answered about Ed, and then it came back, why couldn't the same thing happen to me too? I think about it often. But I also think that part of why Ed was cancer free for that year was to inspire my cousin and I to have the hope, the faith, the strength to know we could get through it. I will always be thankful for that.

On May 7th, 2003, on their 43rd wedding anniversary, Ed had surgery to have another tumor removed. We were hoping that prayers would help this time just like the last time. He would spend a month in the hospital this time. He would lose a lot of weight too. I was told by this time he was 80 pounds less than when I had seen him last. I could not imagine.

I wish I could end Ed's story there but I can't. And I thought about waiting until later to tell you what happened, but I imagine you are already wondering.

Most of the rest of the year was spent in and out of hospitals. Ed never was well again. My mom's brother died that year right after Thanksgiving. Mary came back for the funeral. When she returned to Colorado, she was in the hospital too. She got very sick and seemed she had a silent heart attack. At this time Ed was again in the hospital. I said so many prayers for this wonderful family. I felt helpless.

I wanted to go out and see them. I wanted him to know I loved him. I wanted to tell him. But yes, I know he knew that because I also always told them any time I talked to them.

Mary did get out of the hospital.

Ed died three days after Christmas that year. I was devastated. I didn't even find out until I emailed my cousin to see how he was.

I got an email back saying the funeral was that Wednesday. I was speechless. Somehow we were never notified that he had died. By the time we found out, there was no way I could get to Colorado to the funeral. I not only was dealt the blow that Miracle Ed was gone, but that I was not able to go and tell him goodbye or to go to the funeral to be there for my aunt.

I called Mary as soon as I heard. We sobbed together on the phone. She told me he knew I loved him and that if I had came out there, he wasn't like I remembered. That I should remember the Ed I knew. I still was crushed that I couldn't go. I still think about that sometimes.

And I always think of Ed. His kindness, his love for all of his family, his gentle soul. Sometimes I will smell his pipe smoke and I will think of him. I could never ever forget my Miracle Ed.

Chapter 35

Sunday, May 18, 2003. Life was very busy at this time getting ready for the Relay. We were doing fundraisers, Kayla was making bracelets to sell and doing very well. It was our first year for a team, so it was a learning year for all of us.

I got my invitation to the survivors' reception to be held right before the Relay. Following that would be the survivor's lap. I was anxious to take part in that. It felt good knowing I could tell the world I was a survivor!

I found out that I had to give a speech the night of Relay. That is something they ask the honorary chair to do. I was writing it in my head on the way home one night. I tend to do that a lot. I always hope by the time I write it down that it will sound half as good as it did in my head. I was actually kind of looking forward to saying a few words to everyone.

Friday, May 23. Almost one year to the date that my world changed forever. I wondered how the day would go. I felt like I was reliving it, just thinking about this 'anniversary' coming up. Then I thought, one year ago , to think, I still had cancer and I didn't even know it yet. (That is truly hard to say!) When I found out, I didn't know what the future held or if there even was one for me. I couldn't imagine what the surgery, the treatments, or anything would be like. I couldn't imagine I would be the one to actually be going through something like this. I had to write a story for the Relay newsletter. I wrote in there that it was the worst, yet best time in my life. And that was very true.

Wednesday, May 28, 2003. One year ago plus one day was the biopsy. I could remember every single minute of it. Actually, I still can to this day. From the 'Let's drain this and get her on her way,' to 'We are going to switch gears a little' and 'I don't expect to make a diagnosis of breast cancer'...... Right. Life could surely throw you some serious curves couldn't it? I was ready for a quiet stress free period in my life.

Saturday, May 31, 2003. Friday I had thought a lot about the year before. 4:10 p.m. when the doctor called and said those words I will never forget. They ran through my head all that weekend. They never stopped at all. "I have some tough news for you."

To think it had been a whole year since then. I found that very hard to believe some days. I was glad it was all gone. I worry always about it coming back. I think anyone who has had cancer and is a survivor will tell you that. I really don't see that ever changing.

Wednesday, June 4, 2003. We were putting all the finishing touches on Relay preparations. Our team had raised over $1400. Not too bad for a first time. Kayla alone made over $230. That's a lot of bracelets.

I got a letter in the mail. It was from the Mason City Women's Club. They had seen the story about me in the paper and wanted me to speak at their general meeting next spring. I said yes. I figured I had a lot of time to prepare. I considered it an honor.

Friday, June 6, 2003. My very first time for the Relay for Life. The evening started with the survivor's reception. We all got a star medal to wear for the Relay. The youngest survivor there was 34, the oldest 90! After the ceremonies, we went down to the opening ceremonies. The chairperson opened the Relay then introduced me by saying they put out a call for that year's honorary chair and one name stood out-Joy Brown. Wow, I was humbled. I went up on stage. Brian put a medal around my neck. I was surprised, but loved it. I had my Kleenex ready for my speech, just in case. But I did better than I thought I would. Especially when I looked out and even before I started, I could see my team members-friends and family-already tearing up. My cousin Jennifer cries very well!

I would like to share my speech with you. I kept it short as I knew we had a lot to do.

"Good evening. My name is Joy Brown. I want to welcome everyone here and tell you first how humbled I am to be this year's honorary chairperson. We are all here tonight for the same cause, yet we are here for different reasons. Some of us are here to honor family members who are right now fighting the battle with cancer, some of us are here to honor those who have fought the battle with cancer and have won that battle and some of us are here to honor those who have fought but lost their battle. I am here both to honor my family members but also as one of the survivors. A little over a year ago my world was turned upside down when I got a diagnosis of breast cancer. It was something that I never expected to happen to me. At least not at my age, with four young kids of my own. Suddenly I had to wonder if I would be here for my children's proms, graduations, or even my daughter's first day of middle school...all the things you take for granted that you will be around for. I found myself looking at them wishing to be there for them not only in the future after they are grown but now when I know they need me the most.

Cancer affects people of all ages, taking many far too soon. The money that you have raised will help those who might need a ride to an appointment, it will help women feel better with the Look Good, Feel Good classes, it will help educate, it will help research, and it will hopefully help find the answers that lead to a cure.

My wish tonight is that we won't need this Relay in the future, that my children will never have to agonize over how to tell their own kids that they have cancer and that they will never know the ache of looking at them and wondering if they will get to see them grow up.

On behalf of myself and everyone who has been touched by this disease, I thank you from the bottom of my heart. Have a great Relay and God bless you all!"

I exited the stage, looked around and saw very few dry eyes. One woman who I didn't even know was sobbing and asked me if she could hug me. I of course said yes. I had many compliments during the Relay about my speech and many told me I had made them cry.

Next was the survivor's lap. That was so cool. People would clap for us when we walked around. During the second lap, the family got to join in, so Tom and Kayla walked with me. It was the best lap of the night.

We had a great time, and raised a lot of money. I knew after this first one I was hooked and would be doing this every single year as long as I was able. But then, like I said in my speech, I was also longing for the day that we didn't have to hold the Relays. The day of a cure. The day I would always pray for.

Chapter 36

Sunday, June 15, 2003. Father's Day. Always a bittersweet day for me , having lost my father at such a young age. It had been over 40 years before and I still missed him.

It had been just one year before that I was spending my first night sleeping in my recliner- having just been released from the hospital. What a year it had been since. I couldn't believe all that had happened. All that I had been through. I was so grateful that the year had gone by already and that all the treatments were behind me. I hoped for only checkups ahead for me. I thought of that often. Unpreventable you know, you can't help but think about the future. I wanted to forget for just one day what I had gone through, but I knew that was not possible. There would always be reminders for me. Besides, it really was not something that was ever far from your mind.

Thursday, July 17, 2003. See time was passing and I was back to doing normal things. I didn't post much in my online journal because I figured most weren't checking anymore now that the first year was done and I was back to living my life. I don't think most realized that a hello, I am still thinking of you really would have done wonders for me.

I had gone over to the Charles City Relay for Life and saw my Aunt Alice walk. She is a two-time survivor. I talked to a couple friends of mine from high school.

I had gone to a Goo Goo Dolls/Bon Jovi concert that week in Minneapolis with a couple girls from work. It kicked butt! I loved being there although it meant only a couple hours of sleep that night. Wouldn't you think at a place like this I could go and enjoy myself and not think about what happened to me? Nope. It popped into my head there. It seemed to invade my mind anywhere, any time. I tried to live my normal life, then I would think but for how long? Would it come back. I hated it. I wished there was a button I could hit that would turn all that thinking off.

From my journal, Friday, July 25,2003. 'Good morning. Been one long week. Thanks for the well wishes for our family everyone. For those of you who might be checking and don't know, my stepfather passed away on Monday. It's kind of strange how you can be here one minute, and then you are not. Life is short no matter what! Time flies, you know the sayings….all seem to be true. Anyhow, he is much better off now, as he declined so recently and was miserable….how else do you put it? So we have been at mom's most of the week and will be heading over there often…amazing how much there is to do. Makes me look around here and makes me think. Well, you just never know."

During the rest of the summer we spent most of our time at my mom's going through the house, getting things ready for an auction. It was a difficult job at best. Not only physically, obviously, but emotionally as well.

I will never forget one day when I went outside. Most of the family was taking a break out in the screened in the porch by the garage. I did not go in there. I stopped at the door and looked in. My mom was smoking, and so were my husband, my sister and two brothers in law. I took that in and I was angry. Suddenly the whole thing I went through seemed very unfair. I had never smoked in my life. Never. And I was the one who had had cancer, not any of those five. And it was hard to see. Not only that they were the smokers, not I, but that they could all so easily smoke around me. It kind of hurt.

Checkup time was looming ahead of me already and I was getting nervous all over again.

I had to keep thinking everything was fine. This time I had to have a routine (is anything ever now?) chest x-ray so that added to my anxiety. I don't think I would ever be a fan of any kind of medical test or procedure again.

During this time in the couple of weeks before I had my checkup, I was visiting the online support group again. There had been a lot of people with recurrences and it was scaring the crap out of me, to be honest. There were even some ladies who I had chatted with, who had lost their battle. I would wonder why some could be saved and some couldn't. (It is still something I think about to this day when it comes to breast cancer.) It seemed like every day when I went on there; there was someone who had it again. I actually ended up deleting my bookmark on my computer to that sight. I could not handle reading about it one more time. And I felt bad that I wasn't supporting them at the time but with my checkup being so close I couldn't afford to think of such a possibility for myself. God, this was a hard thing to live with. Everything had changed for me. Nothing anymore was as it was. Nothing. I would never get used to that fact.

Chapter 37

Friday, August 22, 2003. Kayla's summer band concert. Only four songs long. And there I was, sitting all alone before it got started and I choked up. Just because I was there. That surprised me. You would think by then I would be used to reactions like that. I wasn't. I was grateful to be there for something like this and hoped I would be for a long long time.

Thursday. I had a training that evening for a program called Reach for Recovery. It is a program for when women are just diagnosed with breast cancer or have already undergone the surgery. The program matches up those women with women who have already been through it all. It gives them someone to talk to who has been through the same thing as them. Someone who can understand their feelings. A truly invaluable program. I made a vow when I was diagnosed that when I made it through I would help others any way I could. This was just one of those ways.

The next day would be appointment day again. Somehow that evening before I wasn't actually freaking out over it! I still wanted prayers though, from everyone that things would turn out okay.

Friday, August 29, 2003. I had the chest x-ray first. My doctor thought it looked even better than the one I had before surgery the year before. I was shocked. When she overlapped them she thought she saw a little density in the vertebrae and said it was probably arthritis. Probably? Did she know how much I hated that word. I remember that word from a year ago...It Probably wasn't breast cancer either. We all know how that turned out! She asked if I had back pain. Who doesn't? I was hoping at any rate, the radiologists would confirm what she said about it. She thought the radiated side felt pretty darn good and was very pleased. She had to measure my arms. They were still the same so that was also good. You see, since they took those nine lymph nodes, we always will be checking for lymph edema. It can come any time. She asked if my right arm ached a lot when I used it. It did then. It still does. That can be a sign of lymph edema. I told her I put it on a pillow at night, which seemed to help.

Then it was time to see my oncologist. Ugh, I still hate even writing that. 'My oncologist'. No one should have to have one of those!

He ordered the blood work. Told me if it turned out fine, they sent me a letter! What? If he would see anything that needed follow up, he would call me. Did he know just how much I truly hated that? More waiting…..That really should be a four letter word! He did tell me he was sure they would be fine. I wondered how he could know that until he actually saw them. If everything was good, I would return again in December.

When it came to actually going to this checkup, this time was worse than the last one. My mouth got so dry by the time I got there. I had never felt so much anxiety before ever in my life. Not even waiting for the biopsy. Then it didn't seem like a real possibility he would call and tell me I had cancer. But he did. Now the possibility would always loom strong in my mind.

Monday, the first business day after my appointment. Can you guess how I acted every time the phone rang Jumped out of my skin. The doctor didn't call. By Tuesday when he still hadn't called, I figured the blood tests must be fine.

Then Wednesday came. When I got home, Chris handed me a name and number to call. I recognized the hospital prefix and radiation oncology number immediately. I tried to call back and the phones were already turned off for the night. No message left for me, nothing. Just the number. The only thing that 'tried' to ease my mind through the night was that it was the nurse who had actually called me. Remember my rule of thumb don't you? It seems the nurses get to call you when it's good news and doctors will call you when it isn't. But then by now, you know how my mind works. I was still very worried.

Morning finally came after what seemed like a week. I call the number and she is in a meeting! ARGH! She finally called me back at work. She had called to tell me the x-rays were FINE! She apologized for the stress but didn't know who she was talking to and I told her it was my son and that she could have told him. She said she should have left her home phone number. No kidding.

Thursday I was at work and got called to the phone again. I say hello. "Mom? I fell in tennis and blew out my knee again." Oldest son Chris. PE had not been so very good to him. This was the fourth or fifth time it had happened. I decided it would also be the last. By the time I got him to the car to take him to the doctor, he couldn't walk. I got him there, grabbed a wheelchair and got him to the doctor. Who took x-rays. It wasn't broken but he had a big space between his joints that shouldn't be there. So we got to return to orthopedics the next week. He was in a knee mobilizer and had crutches.

The orthopedic doctor thought Chris should have surgery but it could wait until after he graduated. He got that excuse for no more p.e. although I thought it was a few years late. He also had a touch of arthritis in his left knee from all the times this had happened. We actually never did have the surgery and he has improved over the last couple of years.

Saturday, September 27, 2003. Kayla and I walked in our first Walk, Run and Wag for the Cure. It used to be just the Walk and Run for the Cure, but they added the Wag so people could walk with their dogs, too. It was a cold day, but once we got walking it was all right. I saw so many people I knew. Even all of my doctors. It was good to see them there. Found out a couple of them even had personal reasons for being there. I had a thought about how great it was that so many wonderful things could come from something so awful. I felt blessed.

Monday when I got to work, one of the managers brought me back a package that had come in the mail there for me. It was from the district manager's secretary. In it was a wonderful card and an angel of courage. She had said she had just been thinking about me and all I had been through. I was surprised but very touched by her gesture. It still sits on my end table where I can always glance at it and get that little boost of courage any time I might still need it.

Chapter 38

Thursday, October 16, 2003. Tom had gotten a call the night before that his cousin had died. She had been diagnosed with cancer and went pretty quick. I did get to meet her once a couple years before that. Anyhow, I still hated this disease and still planned on always being involved in fighting it. But I thought, wouldn't it be nice if that weren't necessary.

Sunday, November 2. Remember when I told you that they wanted me to speak at the Mason City Women's club in April? Their November speaker broke some bones and cancelled, so they now wanted me to speak on November 11th. Yikes. April sounded like a lot to time for which to prepare for. Just over a week away.... didn't sound like enough.

I found out that I was to talk for 30-60 minutes and it would be in front of about 100 people. Was I freaking out a bit? Yes! I wondered how I ever was going to be able to talk that long.

Tuesday, November 11, 2003. Early morning. I was thinking I would be glad when it was later and the speech was over. My mother in law had come over on the Saturday before and says to me, "I hear you are speaking." What? Seems after all these years of living here, she was invited to join this club and to attend the meeting the day I was speaking. That put an interesting twist on it all.

The speech actually went very very well. I actually talked for 35 minutes. I wasn't nervous but of course thought I could do better. As I was talking I saw a lot of people wiping tears and I even made them laugh a few times. Dare I say it? I LOVED it! I thought that maybe I should do more of that.

I won't put the speech here as it is a condensed version of what you have been reading here. At least up to the point of where I spoke. But the story didn't end there, it continues on.

Wednesday, November 26, 2003. I wrote in my journal: "What were you all doing one year ago today? I know what I was doing! Finishing up treatment!!! It was my very last one after a very long time of them. I cannot believe it has been so long. Time flies. A year ago I could not begin to think about a year later. Oh, I wanted it, to be that far out, to have hair again, to be back to a normal life again. Okay, I can hear you all out there saying my life has never been normal and while that is true, it has been MY normal. So here I am!!!!!!! I have another checkup in two weeks.... gosh, didn't I just do that? So start those prayers anytime. I want to thank you all for hanging in there with me. I am thankful for ALL of you. Now, what are YOU thankful for????"

Wednesday, December 3, 2003. I was trying to stay healthy amongst so many sickies out and about. My checkup was the 12th and you couldn't have a cold or it would mess up the blood count. I didn't want that to happen in any way shape or form. I just wanted this one done and behind me too. I then had my one year checkup at the plastic surgeon. I couldn't believe it had been a year for that already too. I knew I would probably be facing some more surgery to realign the implants or make them better because they were not good. I hated the thought of being put under again, but couldn't leave them like they were.

My uncle Roy had passed away the week before. He was my mom's brother. I was thinking how we always talked about how time flies. It seemed like only yesterday when we were young kids, going to my Grandma's for Christmas and all our aunts and uncles and cousins would be there. And now we were all older and many of them were no longer with us. It made me incredibly sad.

Wednesday, December 10, 2003. I wasn't in a very good mood. I had been reflecting back on the last two years in my life. Three of us in the family had been diagnosed with cancer, my stepfather died, my uncle died, my aunt got sick on the way home from his funeral and was put in the hospital along with my Uncle Ed. I thought our family could use some prayers. Just because.

Friday, December 12, 2003. Had some good news and some GREAT news to share with everyone. I had my checkup and everything went fine. The doctor even had some of my blood tests in his hand by the time he came into the room. Trust me, that is a whole lot better than having to wait for a letter and no phone call, please! He said they were fine! He still had the liver enzyme one to wait for, which is the ultra-sensitive one that picks up anything going on, even if you have a drink the day before! The BEST thing he said to me that day? I didn't have to go back for SIX months!!! Not four. But SIX! I felt glad, happy, scared. He said since I had no positive nodes it didn't make sense to have me living my life and then coming in there and doing that so often. Thank you! I still had to go to the radiation one every four months for two years which was fine with me. They just watched my skin and tissue. But the next November, that would go to six months, too and I would only have to go in there twice a year.

Life was good.

Wednesday, December 31, 2003. My 18th anniversary. That was hard to believe. We weren't going to be doing much. The year before I was recuperating from surgery. And speaking of that. I was scheduled for another one. January 9th. Why you may ask? Well, if I can be blunt. The implants I had were too small. I was scheduled for bigger boobs! I had so much fun telling the guys I knew that. Even my boss at the time. Problem was some people took it that I was going to have surgery again JUST because I wanted bigger boobs? Oh dear NO! The ones I had, we found out ran small and one of them seemed smaller than the other, like it had flattened on the bottom. So they were too small for my frame and height. I looked quite flat chested. My husband, the comedian he always is, got quite a lot of mileage out of this one and getting to pick out bigger ones. I still say, you just gotta laugh!

It was also at this time that I had gotten the news that Uncle Ed had passed away on Sunday. One of his daughters had been out of town and she got the call to get home. He hung on until she made it home to say goodbye. Then he was gone. I still sting from this loss. When I went to work and told my boss , he said, "Oh girl, your family……" No kidding. I still regret never getting out there to see him or say goodbye.

Chapter 39

Tuesday, January 6, 2004. I finally got a call from the hospital. I had to arrive for surgery at 7:45 a.m with surgery scheduled for 9:15. At least the wait from check in to surgery was supposed to be less this time.

I was getting a bit nervous about being put under again. I was asking for those good thoughts and prayers, as I knew how much they helped. I made sure that no one forget to include the surgeon and anesthesiologist in their prayers too!

Surgery day finally came. At 8:30 the nurse still hadn't come into my room to do all of her prep before surgery, that was to happen in 45 minutes. But the anesthesiologist had. He told me that during my last surgery I was hard to intubate. No one had told me that! It was probably something that was good to know. He proceeded to tell me what they would do this time, paused and asked me if I was nervous. Well if I wasn't before I truly was after that! The nurse finally showed up, as did the doctor to do his drawing. The surgical nurse came to take me down and she had to wait because they hadn't even put in the IV yet. So at a little before nine, I was yet again walking into the operating room.

This time they had given me Verset to 'relax' me first. I will tell you I really HATE that stuff. It makes everything spin. Everything in the room was moving. I felt like I was watching the highway lines go by at high speed. Ick.

Finally they had me breathe oxygen and I was out. I woke up in recovery and the doctor was actually there. I heard a nurse say, "That looks nasty." Great. Now what? Seems my IV got infiltrated so they had to take it out. After only twenty minutes in recovery they took me back to my room. I got sick afterwards like I always did, so they had to put the IV back in for Zofran. It took more than one attempt to get that IV back in. I dozed off and on until about 3pm and woke up and asked for a piece of toast. I got to sit in the chair around 4 and went home shortly after that. (I decided then that you know you have been in the hospital too many times when everyone starts to recognize you!)

When you go to the surgery waiting room, you have to tell them who you are there with and how you are related. Now remember Tom was the ONLY one who came with me that day.

When he got there and checked in the volunteer told him, "Oh her dad already checked in and is in there." He said, "Now that would be some trick!" (Remember my dad died when I was 4) He did go to where she said this man was and of course there was no man sitting there. At least not one he could see! Did he ask her what he looked like? Of course not!

The first day home, I was all alone. I tried to sleep and the pain pills helped some. But wouldn't you know, every time I fell asleep, the phone would ring. People wanting to know how I was. I figured if they would have just let me sleep, I would feel better.

I had to return to get stitches out in two weeks. Oh and in case, you were wondering, yes, they looked a whole lot better. I was glad. I didn't want any more surgery for awhile.

Tuesday, January 13, 2004. I had a Relay meeting, a financial aid meeting as my oldest graduated that year and would be on to college, and Oh I did some smoozing too. With let's see, our old vice president, Al Gore, Martin Sheen, Rob Reiner and Senator Tom Harkin, who called me a pioneer for fighting for inclusion for so long. I went back to work the day before. Not must time off. I needed the money. The boss thought I could do more than I was allowed. Sometimes he just didn't understand.

I got my stitches out on Thursday the 22nd. Then Sunday night came.

At about 10:30 on Sunday night, I was laying in bed watching television. For some reason, I noticed something in the left implant was just not right. I thought maybe it had moved. I panicked a little. I went into the bathroom to look and I could see it hadn't moved, but suddenly it was growing larger right before my eyes! I looked like it was swelling. I woke Tom up and told him something was wrong. I called the hospital's after hours number. They asked me if I could hold. I said NO! So I didn't. I told them what was going on and they told me to come right in.

I had my pajamas on so I had to throw some jeans on. By this time Tom has to help me because I cannot bend over as it has swollen up so much. It was starting in the armpit, too. I had my shoes half on and could only throw my coat over my shoulder.

Tom drove 70mph even through town and we didn't see one police car. When you get to the ER you usually have to sign in and wait until they get to you. But they took one look at me and took me right in and then right back to the trauma area. Then they paged my doctor. He told them to go ahead and give me a pain killer. A shot. It made me throw up. They tried to take blood in the meantime, had to start an IV, which nobody can manage to hit my veins anymore, since now they only can use my left arm. I felt like a pin cushion by the time they were all done. I had to give more blood for blood type. I told them I was O+ and if they needed blood, to just ask Tom, he was the same type.

The doctor finally came in, told me he never expected to see me in the ER. Well, I didn't expect to be there, either. He told me it was arterial bleeding. That maybe a clip from the mastectomy had come loose and it was now bleeding into my chest wall. Every time that my heart would beat, out more blood came. That was why it was filling up so fast. He wanted to wait until morning to operate because he wanted his own team with him. WHAT? He wanted people he was familiar with to work with. I figured fixing me was more important.
He told me the area would fill up with blood and that would fill up the space and then act as a tourniquet. It didn't give me much comfort. He would go in, in the morning, clean the area, take out the clot, cauterize what was causing this, but if he couldn't see what it was, he would put in a drain. He told me that this had only happened once before to a patient of his.

They put me in a room for the night and surgery was scheduled for 7:30am. I was hoping I would still be around for it.

What I liked this time, was the anesthesiologist listened to me and he gave me stuff so that I wouldn't get nauseous when I woke up. It was the first time in many surgeries where I didn't throw up when I woke up. It was a relief.

The doctor couldn't find the actual vein that was the culprit causing all of this. So he ended up cauterizing FIVE of them. And he put in another drain. I was going to be out of commission for at least another week with that. I was so tired of not being able to do anything, but even more so of all the medical garbage I was yet again going through.

It was very very scary first, not knowing what was happening to me, then knowing and having him talk about bleeding and clots. A lot runs through your mind. I was literally praying to God that I would be around in the morning because I really was worried about that!

I couldn't go do Kayla's birthday shopping, I missed a Relay meeting, I missed work. The interruption of life was tough.

Jamie walked up to me one morning, while I was in my robe, no makeup on, hair not done, nothing. He looked at me. Said "Where's Mom?" At that point, I wasn't quite sure myself.

Chapter 40

Monday, February 2, 2004. We were all snowed in. Except Tom, he went to work while the rest of us stayed home. It was Kayla's birthday and she was sick. I was supposed to go the next day to get my drain out. I was ready for that. I wanted to get back to normal.
I developed a huge rash from the antibiotics from surgery so I was dealing with that too.

Wednesday, February 4, 2004. The last day before I had to go back to work. Being it was Iowa in the winter, it was real nice not having to go anywhere. I did have the drain removed the day before. I was so paranoid that night worrying about the same thing happening all over again. I would think, that doesn't feel right, or should they be this far up, or should I feel them so much, and on and on it went. I had hoped that went away fast.

Tuesday, February 10, 2004. I had returned to work on Thursday. I picked the worst day of my schedule to go back, but I needed the money.

I got my stitches out this day. The doctor thought everything looked good. I had told him I never wanted to go through that again. I had to return in four weeks for a post-surgery check. It would have been sooner, but I had to go four weeks after the most recent one.

Monday night was our Relay for Life kickoff for 2004. We had a speaker that I shall never forget. He was 32 years old. Remember that. 32. He was battling cancer for the SIXTH time! It was very humbling to think about that. I didn't like going through it once, couldn't imagine the nightmare of twice. But SIX times? Wow. He had a great attitude, which is such an amazing thing. I am not sure I would still have a great one if I had to go through it as many times as him. He said something that night that I will never forget. Something like, cancer can never beat him. It could kill him. But it could never beat him, it couldn't change who he was and it could not change his spirit. It could not touch his soul. I understood. I agreed.

We had taken a quilt our team had made. It was made up of Relay t-shirts. We took markers and let people sign it. They would put names of people they were honoring, survivors and those who were not. Some people liked to just sign their name. That was okay too. We took it around to many places we went, set up tables and let people do that. We sold chances for just $2.00 each for a chance to win it the night of the Relay. Which this year, would be the exact two year anniversary of my first surgery to remove the tumor.

Friday February 20, 2004. I just plain hurt. I was wondering why the hell did he put such a 'large' size in? I felt like the implants were trying to break out of the skin. The arm was more numb than before and I wondered if the new larger size wasn't somehow pushing on something and responsible for that.

Thursday February 26, 2004. Happy Birthday to me! I really didn't like getting older much before. Since my diagnosis, I consider every birthday a gift. Adding another year is a good thing.

Wednesday March 3, 2004. I was supposed to go to Clear Lake for a mini kickoff there, but I had gotten a call from the high school nurse and Jamie's teacher. Jamie had had a good day. Then someone coughed and he threw himself onto the floor. Hard. Twice. They were worried about a concussion because he hit his head so hard. So I had to stay home and check on him. I knew writing this in my journal, that some might think, 'poor Joy to have a 'kid like that'. Never mind me. It wasn't about me, it was about Jamie. I just thought how hard it must be for him sometimes.

Tuesday March 9, 2004. My after surgery checkup. It was quick and everything was healing fine. That was great, but some days I was so uncomfortable. More than I ever had imagined I would be. When someone is faced with reconstruction after a mastectomy, I truly feel that they should be told all about it. It really isn't so easy. It isn't a matter of here we shall put these in and you will be a woman again. When I faced it, I was simply told that I was young, I should still look like a woman. Which of course I didn't argue with. I couldn't imagine looking otherwise. I just wish someone could have told me the pros and cons and that some days it was an uncomfortable unnatural feeling, at best.

Wednesday, March 17, 2004. Tom had yet another funeral home to visit. The wife of one of his co-workers died suddenly. She had a heart attack. She was younger than me. Someone there, actually said to him, 'Just think Tom, this could have been you a couple years ago.' I can't quite imagine saying something like that to anyone. Yes, it could have been him. Of course we were truly glad it wasn't for the obvious reason. But I was thinking, you just never really know. You know that old cliché? Yup this one again...That life is too short? Well, it is, so hug those loved ones. Tell them you love them. Be nice to each other. Because you know what? Life IS too short!

Chapter 41

Saturday, April 3, 2004. I wasn't writing in my journal much anymore. Truth be told, I didn't know if anyone was really checking in much. It is funny how the further away from diagnosis you get, it seems people tend to forget. I guess they feel you don't need them anymore. Some might be surprised to know how much sometimes you still do.

Between being so tired I could hardly see straight and my arm giving me such grief, I would come to my journal, look at it and think, maybe tomorrow. Which as you know, never comes! Since the last two surgeries, my arm had hurt more than ever. It got tired quite easily. Sometimes I could hardly get my fingers to work right to even pick things up. It seemed like I could do much less than I could before. I had to put my arm up at night a lot more too. "If I knew then what I know now...." I would think.

Wednesday, April 14, 2004. I had a check up at the radiation oncology department since those were still every 4 months. Those were usually not too bad and didn't cause the anxiety like the other ones where they draw my blood.

I want to tell you now a little bit about something that started during all of this. It is something that my daughter and I share in to this day. During this time, a show called American Idol started. We got hooked during auditions when this redheaded guy from North Carolina came out and started singing. I couldn't believe that voice came out of him! From that moment we voted every week. Of course you all know I am speaking of Clay Aiken. He didn't 'win' in that he didn't get the title on finale night, but he has won in every sense of the word since.

Kayla and I had a great experience of April 16th, 2004 thanks to the generosity of several people. We went to St. Paul to see Clay in concert. We rode up with a lady who got us tickets when she got hers. Kayla and I got to go to the pre-party thanks to someone we had never met until that night. We had a lot of fun. We stood in the t-shirt line at the concert for an hour and then barely made it to our seats in time for Clay to enter. The lights dimmed,, and screams like you cannot believe were heard. Then his voice, and he entered from the back of the arena. It is a moment I will never forget. I looked over at Kayla and she is wiping tears from her eyes. I put my arm around her. She told me later that she was just so glad to be there. So was I. So was I.

Since this time, we have seen Clay many many times. Each time is a special memory and each time I am grateful to be here to be able to share this with my daughter. We have met so many people because of Clay and have had so many opportunities. We have got on planes and got to dip our toes in the ocean for the very first time.

Before May 31, 2002, I am not so sure we would have done any of this. Going through such a diagnosis and realizing we are not guaranteed any amount of time on this earth , well, it can really change your life. I chose to let it change mine for the better. So even to this day, we continue to go to Clay concerts and have a great time. As long as he is singing, we will be sharing in it.

He also has a voice that soothes me when I am anxious. On the way to every checkup, I will play a Clay cd. I remember going to one checkup that was particularly making me more nervous than before, I was playing my music like always. Bridge Over Troubled Water was on. As I pulled into my parking spot, the words he sang....."I WILL EASE YOUR MIND!" That was the

last thing I heard before I turned off the car.
I knew at that moment I could get through my
appointment. And I did.

And I have to thank that redhead from North
Carolina for making a difference in my life,
to bringing fun back to me again, and giving
my daughter and I such great and wonderful
memories.

Wednesday, May 5, 2004. Real life was
keeping me very very busy. I had a graduation
to plan. My oldest was graduating in just over 3
weeks. I said a prayer of thanks to be able to be
here planning for that.

Kayla's story was in the paper. They wrote
about how she was making bracelets and selling
them to make money for her Relay team. They
talked about the hundreds she had made and
how they were sent all over the world. They
talked about the reason why she was doing
this. The survivor's committee from the Relay
even put in an order of 100 to give away to the
survivor's that night. The paper wrote about her
in an editorial after that and her teachers wrote
a letter to the paper talking about her and the
example she was. She continues to this day to
fight hard for the cause, even winning an award
from the American Cancer Society called the
Sword of Hope Award. First one they gave out...

and she won it, at age 12! I couldn't be more proud of her!

Thursday, June 10, 2004. One day until Relay. Graduation done. Only three more to go! Eleven more days to go until my next 6 month checkup. Yes, I was getting nervous. As usual, I just wanted to get it over with.

Thursday, June 22, 2004. Relay had been a wonderful success. We had to hold it inside due to rain. Kayla's team made over $1000, most of that being from her!! She had brought her Clay cd so they would play her favorite song from it during the night. "Shine". So appropriate for her! While they played it, she had been sleeping because she didn't' feel so good so she missed it. But when she woke up, they played it again for her. (And this part still surprises me. The guy playing all the music never mentioned who sang the songs, but when this song was done, he said, 'That was Clay Aiken and he is going to be at the Iowa State Fair on August 15th. Tickets go on sale this morning.'! All true, but made me think he must have daughters!)

I had got through another checkup. The doctor read the blood tests and said "Excellent, perfect!" Back in 6 months. Four days before Christmas. Didn't like that. Although the nurse said, I had to know that one would be okay, right

before Christmas. Whatever you say! I think
I would hold her to that.

    I only checked in on my journal once more
that summer. I guess I didn't go there much
because there really wasn't a lot to tell. That was
a good thing, I thought. It meant that life was
somewhat back to normal. My normal anyhow.
I had a radiology checkup in August but that was
pretty much it for me. And I liked it. I never forgot
the summer two years before. I preferred this one.

Chapter 42

Life returned to normal pretty much, after that. Normal for me. I still have my checkups every 6 months. It seems the more I have, the more anxious I get. I am not sure why. I want to have a BIG number before the word 'survivor' I guess. I want cancer to never return. I never forget how it was to hear I had it when the doctor called me in 2002. Sometimes I still hear those words in my mind. I never want to hear them out loud again.

My last visit caused so much anxiety that I called and got in three days early. I couldn't wait any longer than that. I had a lot of waiting that day and it was tough. I walked out again with everything being okay. I said my prayer of thanks.

I say one every day actually. Today outside, the weather is gorgeous, the sun is shining. I walked to the post office for work and when I was returning, that same line that the husband of Jamie's preschool teacher said, popped into my mind again. "I am not afraid of dying. I am afraid of not existing." I thought at this moment walking and enjoying this weather and FEELING the sun and the wind was one of those reasons. I am also afraid of not existing. I cannot imagine not being here to put my arm around my daughter when she needs it, to share in the things we have shared, whether it would be shopping or going to a concert or just hanging out. I cannot imagine not being here, meeting my sons first real girlfriend, or helping him through a tough time with college. I cannot imagine not being here sharing my birthday every year with my youngest son, and enjoying the gentle soul he is. I cannot imagine not being here for Jamie, to help him make his way through this world, to make sure people don't take advantage of him, and yes to protect him. I cannot imagine not laughing, crying, loving, hurting. I cannot imagine not enjoying music, art, literature. I cannot imagine not existing.

But in your mind, you think about it. You wonder what it would be like for everyone. How my kids so young would go on. How my husband would be able to handle everything. How it would be like for them not to have me here.

That is part of my normal now. So is worrying about every little pain. I turn my head, if it hurts, well, it must have went there. If I cough, oh dear, now it went there. Is it logical? Probably not. But it's a very human thing to do. I don't like it. I don't want to worry about it. I pray I will be fine. What else can you do.

I use the cliché's often when I talk to people. You know....one especially....Life is too short. And you never know, so hug those you love, and tell them. Oh and don't sweat the small stuff. The time wasted on it just isn't worth it. Live your life like you want to. Trust yourself. Find the joy.

What I went through was an altering experience in all ways. If you did not know me and met me, you would never know by looking at me what I had gone through. I have hair again, I look like a girl. So why would you know? I don't wear a sign that says "Breast Cancer Survivor." Although, I do wear a couple pink bracelets for the cause and occasionally the pin. But so do a lot of people.

I have been altered physically. The obvious of course by the double mastectomy and subsequent reconstruction. But also by everything the chemo and radiation can do. There are worries of course. Did you know chemo can weaken the heart? Did you know these treatments can cause the very disease they are trying to get rid of? I live with a weakened right arm, sometimes it just aches so much. I still hate that I am not able to do everything I used to and everything I want to. I sometimes feel this disease and its treatment took more than just body parts from me. I get angry sometimes, I cry still sometimes. Not so often anymore. But yes, sometimes I long for those days before May

31,2002. Who wouldn't? I long for the days of not worrying about recurrence and not yelling at the tv because I cannot stand one more story about cancer and I just want them to shut up for once.

I took something horrible and have tried to make the best out of it. I do that with all the adversity in my life. I made that vow to make a difference, to help others and I am still trying to do that. Whether it is by sending a card, lending an ear or working tirelessly for the cause, I hope that someday when I no longer exist, someone will remember me not for all the bad things I had to endure, but for the good I made out of them. I hope that I made a difference for just one.

I almost didn't write my story. I will tell you why. I was afraid. Not to tell it. But to be done with it. I thought, what if that is what God had in store for me. And that was all he needed me for and then, when my story was done, so would I be. But you know what, I figured out, this story continues on and even though I may be done with this one that you are reading, I do know it isn't the end of my story at all.

I have come through the greatest pain in my life, but also the time of my greatest joy. I have new hair, a new life. The me I was for so long is no longer. But you know what? I love the me I am!

Chapter 43

May 2009. It's been a little while since I wrote this, and I just wanted to add one more chapter to my story. When time has passed as it has, things continue to change, stories continue on.

I am 7 now. As of my last birthday. That is what I tell people. This new me, is 7. I can hardly believe it. I have had 7 birthdays since my diagnosis 7 years ago this week. 7 years of other birthdays, two more graduations, with one to go! My little girl, who was 10? She will be finishing high school and graduating next year! Time really does fly.

We have lost a few more people too. My mom's friend who sent me that wonderful card I told you about. And my mom. She passed away in December of 2007. I miss her always and find it a bit sad she will not be able to read my story. But then I think, maybe that is a good thing, maybe it would have been too much for her to read. We have also lost my husband's Uncle, Aunt and his mother in December 2008. Life continues to change for us, causing , always it seems, new adjustments.

I have 'graduated' to checkups once a year. That was exciting, and again scary. A whole year in between. Seems a lot of time when 'stuff' can happen. I had my first one after the first year last month. I was so so nervous, so scared. I was thrilled and relieved once again when I heard my tests were 'wonderful'. When you are no longer on medicine of any kind and treatments are long behind you, it is even scarier! I have tried to change my eating habits for the better, knowing it does make a difference in my health. And a bonus , is I am slimmer than ever. Not bad for an old broad! I am trying to exercise more. I did find too, that when I lost weight, some of the aches and pains from my implants and arm improved immensely. I considered some further surgery to take out radiated tissue and change the right implant with fat from my stomach, but when it came right down to it, I could not go through with another surgery. Maybe in the future, just not now.

So my story continues. I do worry, I still think about the future. I don't think that will ever change. I do find some days, I can almost not think about what happened. Almost. I have those physical reminders that never go away. Some days I still struggle with that. But all that said, I still find the joy. I STILL know that life is too short.

If you come away with just one thing from my story, I hope it is...Find the joy. Truly. I hope you find yours in each and every day. This life stuff can get pretty hard at times, but it is pretty amazing too!

Made in the USA
Lexington, KY
23 November 2009